The

Sin

Paradox

The

Sin

Paradox

The Case Against Adam, Eve, and the Serpent

D B Evans

©2018

ISBN: 979-8-9880156-0-4 (sc)

ISBN: 979-8-9880156-2-8 (hc)

ISBN: 979-8-9880156-1-1 (e)

Library of Congress Control Number: 2019907219

Jamaer Productions rev. date: 3/1/2023

1212B Thornbury Ln
Manchester, NJ 08759
www.jamaerproductions@gmail.com

This is dedicated to all those who want to know God better. Those who are not content with the typical platitudes and shallow answers to questions yet unresolved. As Thomas Jefferson stated: "*Question with boldness even the existence of a God; because, if there be one, he must more approve of the homage of reason, than that of blind-folded fear.*"

So, dare to ask the hard questions, do not settle for empty platitudes. Keep asking, but be patient, the answers do not always come the moment we ask. One day the Lord may just allow you to have the answers you seek. It may come from a person, a book or a simple word whispered to your spirit late one night.

"For I seek not to understand in order that I may believe, but I believe in order that I may understand. For I believe for this reason: that unless I believe, I cannot understand."

Anselm,

A special thank you goes out to all who have stood by me in the development of this book. To our Father in Heaven my earthly mother with Him, and my father on earth all who I owe all that I am. To my wife Teri, for enduring the late nights. To all my family and friends. Thank you all for having supported and encouraged me throughout my life and during the writing of this thesis.

Contents

Preface

I will be presenting a new and very controversial theory. So, before reading this thesis a few things need to be mentioned. I tend to use the name Yeshua which is the name Jesus would have been called when He walked the earth. Its meaning is "God's Salvation" or "Salvation". It is not anything against using the English version "Jesus", it's just become more of my own habit. When you look at the Hebrew words and names, they have a much deeper meaning than the translations or transliterations. More examples of this will be seen later.

I will also tend to use the word messiah instead of Christ for the same reason. Both words do mean "the anointed" but it's not an exact match or translation. When the Septuagint was written the Hebrew scholars had to use the best or most accurate Greek word they could find to translate from the original Aramaic or Hebrew text. The word "Christos" was the closest word in the Greek to that of the Hebrew "Mashiach".

Yes, both mean "anointed" but messiah or rather "Mashiach" means the anointing is poured on, as they did when anointing a king. The olive oil was poured on the new monarch. The word "Christos" from where we get the word "Christ" means more as the oil is being "rubbed in" as opposed to "poured on". It may seem as though it's being a little bit picky but like the use of the name Yeshua, it's become a habit and maybe more a personal preference at this point than any kind of intended theological statement. I have no problem using the name Jesus or the word Christ. I've just come to use the phrase Messiah Yeshua or Yeshua ha Mashiach more often and thus it has become a habit of mine at this time.

Another point is the axiom of there being no such thing as a "coincidence" in the Bible. Everything is intended to be there stated just the way it is, usually for multiple reasons. These reasons may include references to the current events of that time as well as prophetic future events.

They may be in relation to specific similarities in Biblical persons, such as those who proceed and represent attributes of the coming Messiah. The point being everything in the Bible is written there for a reason. It's within those reasons, along with the language, specific words used and phrases as well as other elements that the lessons, information and answers to questions are contained. It is also within all those elements the Biblical patterns show up.

Context

An important aspect of interpretation is context. Any Bible passage should first be taken in its original context. This is true as it gives a base line for interpreting that passage. However, if only the original context were to be used, there would be no prophecy, no repeated patterns or types.

These repeated patterns and types are a core element of Biblical interpretation. How it all plays to future events is the more difficult part of interpretation. To glean prophecy accurately a student must seek other similar passages and references outside of the confines of the original context of a verse or chapter, or book for that matter. Since the Bible is used to look forward in seeking prophecy's warnings and signs, the question becomes, can we then also look backwards?

The answer to this is a simple "yes", of course we can. Today scholars look back to when the Bible was written and reflect on the surrounding historical settings. When the Bible was written down it already was looking backwards to the origins of Creation. When authenticating Yeshua's credentials to be the prophesied Messiah, all of the Tanakh must be gone through. It is only in those books that the credentials, authority and attributes of Messiah are detailed.

As a result, it is not only possible, it's required to use the same typology and repeated patterns to look back and try to understand how a particular pattern or type may have started. This concept is at the core of this thesis; the process of unwinding the types and patterns to their beginnings. In this case it is the pattern of sin.

This thesis will try and do just that, unwind or reverse the patterns and types to their beginnings. There is a lot to uncover and discover along the way. Studying the Bible is always a journey of discovery.

One last point to bring up is the concept of thinking outside the box. To try and look at some of these familiar passages in a different light, in a new way. At no point am I trying to change their known meaning, it is more like adding another layer to those layers which already exist. As mentioned, what will be presented can be considered a very controversial theory. Please keep an open mind until the end, think a little "outside the box".

"Understanding is the reward of faith. Therefore, understand not that you may believe, but believe that you may understand"!

Augustine of Hippo

par·a·dox

per ə ˌ däks

noun: paradox; plural noun: paradoxes

a seemingly absurd or self-contradictory statement

or proposition that when investigated or explained

may prove to be well founded or true.

*It is the glory of God to conceal a matter
and the glory of kings to search it out.
(Prov. 25:2 TLV)*

Introduction

This book has been years in the making. Once the inspiration was given to me, I could not get away from the idea. It was an answer to a question I had had for quite some time. I then found it to appear throughout history, everyday life today and most importantly all throughout the Bible. Were these all just coincidences? But as mentioned, in the Bible there's no such thing as a "coincidence".

Since this is based on the Bible, it is primarily only the Bible which can decipher the clues and lead one to the conclusion presented. Due to the nature of the conclusion the supporting evidence had to be overwhelming and not a mere opinion. However, this did not start as an opinion but a revelation. Then the work started, the supporting evidence had to be gathered and compiled. As this was done the conclusion was increasingly more obvious. I was surprised how much corroborating evidence there was.

On Biblical interpretation there are some basic rules. First and foremost is the Bible must interpret itself. Our interpretation cannot interpret the Bible. That is what I've tried to do. Let Biblical passages point the way.

There are also multiple levels used to interpret the Bible. Two of the methods used from ancient sages and Rabbis to today are the Parshat or written word as it stands on its own and the Remez or the clues contained in the words and phrases used by the writer of a particular book. These would then be cross referenced across all the other books of the Bible to gain better understanding of the words and phrases being used.

Along with these is the use of the ancient pictographs representing specific Hebrew letters which make up a word. An interesting dynamic of Hebrew are the meanings contained within the Hebrew letters. Each of the 22 letters have a special meaning of their own which when combined encapsulates the meaning of the word. It's not an exact match or definition but rather the essence of the word they make up. When bringing all these elements of interpretation together a larger picture of people, events and meanings can be seen.

The methodology does not stop there. Throughout the Bible are recurring themes, patterns and what are called "types". The character of Messiah is portrayed throughout the Scripture in the ways and characters of a variety of Biblical persons. Joseph, son of Jacob, represents the suffering servant. Moses depicting the greatest of the prophets and bearer of the instructions, laws of God. David as the conquering king. Solomon as the wisest of rulers. All these individuals and more from the Bible depict various traits and character elements of the one who will come, the Messiah Yeshua.

In making the case against Adam, Eve and the Serpent, we need to ask some questions pertinent to the topic which include the following.

- ➤ What did Adam and Eve actually do?
- ➤ What specific kind of fruit was it?
- ➤ Why did Satan take the form of a serpent?
- ➤ Why did Satan do it? What were his motives?
- ➤ Why did Jesus / Yeshua have to die?
- ➤ Why did He have to die the way He did?
- ➤ Why did the last days of Yeshua's life play out the way they did?
- ➤ How does the sinful act of Adam and Eve permeate all of subsequent human existence

and actions such as wars, debt, greed and all the other sins mankind experiences?

➢ How are the punishments appropriate to the crime?

➢ How could their act of sin affect all of Creation itself?

With these and more in mind, as you read through this thesis many similar questions will arise. Many I'm sure have asked these same questions in their own mind at times, usually all beginning with the word "why". Why did God do this or that in such a way. These are great questions and need to be asked if one wants the answer. We may never know all the answers, but we will never know if we never ask.

I grew up in a family full of lawyers and judges, so I saw all this through a modern legalistic courtroom filter. Thus, the question just kept nagging me, "what did they do". What could these two people have done that was so wrong? They had nothing, not even clothes.

I kept asking God "what did they do". Then late one evening when I was studying, working on another unrelated theological thesis, there was a whisper of a single word and it all fell into place and the majority of the conclusions and points in this writing were outlined, eventually ending in the wee hours of the morning.

I sat back, shaking a bit with a tear in my eye, and it all made perfect sense. The feeling or sensation I was experiencing at that moment was mildly electric. Everything I had learned over the years about the various Biblical stories fit. Because of that experience, that single word of knowledge, I knew what happened. All that needed to be done was to flush out all the details and prove the case.

Once it is all brought together, all the means and motives of the crime, as well as some specific details will be easily seen and understood.

It is said, and I agree with the point the Bible is "literally" true. The problem arises when the words used are taken too literally. The Bible is written using metaphors, analogies, poetry as well as straight prose. The problem for the reader is deciphering when each aspect is being used. Some interpreters take the Bible hyper-literally to the point of completely misunderstanding what is being said. The Bible will often use what is called "hyperbole". It's an exaggeration to stress a point. An example of this can be seen in the depiction of those going to John the Baptist to be baptized.

> *Then Jerusalem was going out to him, and all Judea and all the region around the Jordan. (Matthew 3:5 TLV)*

All the Judean countryside was going out to him, and all the Jerusalemites. (Mark 1: 5 TLV)

Does anyone believe ALL of the Judean countryside, all of Jerusalem and the region around the Jordan went to be baptized? Bear in mind this would mean all of those who were not Jews, all the Pharisees, Sadducees, all of the Sanhedrin including the High Priest, the Roman soldiers, the Roman Governor and his court, the Herodian court and all of Herod's guards and soldiers. It is absurd to think this took place like that. The Bible is using hyperbole to stress the point that a great number or percentage of the people went to see John and be baptized. This is what I mean by avoiding "**hyper**-literalism".

Format

The case against Adam, Eve and the Serpent will be presented in four parts with a fifth section of final thoughts on the subject.

The first section will be a simple statement of those involved and related points. It is a short section and serves merely to remind the reader of some of the simple, basic points.

The second section will have the first section restated with more of the relative elements added in.

The third section will be all the details of the case, basically the trial.

The fourth section will be closing arguments. Included in this section will be how this all relates to and permeates both the Old and New Testaments and society in general.

In the end, you are the jury, the judge of the evidence. Not of guilt or innocence of those involved, but whether the evidence which will be presented points to the actual crime committed. Do I make a solid case?

The fifth and final section has some closing thoughts which relate to the conclusions of this thesis.

I have expressed this thesis to several fairly knowledgeable people. Some have flat out said no to the theory. Their reason, they just could not or would not believe it. No evidence, no argument, they could not bring themselves to believe this concept.

Some just did not understand what I was presenting. However, there were some who picked up on it right away and fully agreed with the premise.

There was one who adamantly disagreed, just could not believe it. The person completely changed their mind when I asked why it was so unbelievable. The individual said, "I just cannot believe it because it is the most horrible thing anyone...."; at that point the person stopped talking, looked at me and said, "you may be right". I smiled and nodded my head.

So, I present the case with all the details and facts. Again, I ask for you to withhold judgment until the very end. This book will seek to answer those questions mentioned and more as it works to reconstruct the crime and explain what took place. To do this, a great many fluffy platitudes will need to be stripped away. Some of these are well known such as: "They disobeyed God," or "they ate the fruit", "they ate the apple", "they were tempted", "they listened to the serpent" and so on. These may be true in a sense, but they and others are mostly just shallow conclusions and statements which never get to the heart of the matter, the underlying question, "what did they actually do?".

The different aspects of the crime will be presented. The Commands of God, the disobedience, the punishments, the continuing parallels or "types" which permeate the rest of the Bible will all be presented. It is only through these and other elements can the crime be reconstructed. The perpetrators are already known, their initial punishments are known but not very well understood. What is not known is what did they do to incur the death penalty.

Sin

The word "sin" has an interesting background of being an archery-based term. Where the Hebrew word for "sin" is חטאה (hatah, Strong's #2403) literally means "miss the mark", the word contrasts itself with that of the Hebrew word "yara" which means to "hit the mark".

The word "torah" comes from the root word "yara", carrying with it the concept of hitting the mark, only now it includes the Instructions and Teachings of God.

Many in the Church have taught the word Torah means "law", this is a bad translation of the word and a misconception of what the word implies. The word Torah is God's instructions and commands. Sin remains its opposite as in failing to hit the mark of obeying God's instructions or commands.

There is a pattern to sin in the Bible as will be seen. Certain very specific types of sin have a pattern of punishments associated with them. God is very consistent in this way. A few of these patterns will show up over the course of presenting the information in this book.

Chapter 1 in the Beginning
Beresheet

Since the case deals primarily with what took place at the beginning of the Book of Genesis, that is where this will start.

Beresheet = בְּרֵאשִׁית = "b'ray sheet" or "In the beginning", is the first word in the Bible, the Hebrew name for the first Biblical book commonly known as Genesis. It literally means "in the beginning". Starting with Genesis we look at the incident on its face.

> *When the woman saw that the tree was good for food, and that it was a delight to the eyes, and that the tree was desirable to make one wise, she took from its fruit and ate; and she gave also to her husband with her, and he ate. (Gen 3:6 NASB)*

This is all that is stated in Genesis for what took place. A crime was committed. The specific details of the crime are not listed, only implied. It can only be gleaned by using the Bible's described metaphors. The question is, what did they actually do? What was that fruit? What was that overt action which had the ability to condemn mankind to death through God's Righteous Judgment as well as infect creation itself?

"They disobeyed God" is a foregone conclusion. We already know they disobeyed God. The main question is, in what way? How did they disobey God? To simply say "they ate the fruit" does not answer this question of what the actual fruit was.

A great many theologians tend to stop short of thinking this through and end up stating the obvious "they learned the price of disobedience" or "they gained the knowledge of good and evil". These again do not really answer the question, they only describe an outcome. The "fruits" of their decision.

We all know the price of disobedience. As children we get punished for disobeying our parents. But to have a penalty imposed, especially the death penalty, something had to have actually happened. They must have done something which rose to the level of requiring such extreme retribution. A capital punishment requires a capital crime.

I've read several opinions on this subject from both a Christian and Jewish Rabbinic point of view. Most if not all opinions I have found tend to be shallow or just the same empty platitudes mentioned. Some of the speculations said the fruit was a pomegranate, a grape, wheat and several odd guesses. No deep thought or analysis was incorporated.

The term "the fall of man" refers to man, through Adam, falling from grace, immortality and God's blessings and protection to a state of mortality and sinfulness. This distanced mankind from God.

Two people, supposedly the first two humans imbued with the Spirit (breath) of God did something so heinous it demanded God to invoke the death penalty for them and all their generations. (These generations would not have come about if the death penalty would have been imposed at that moment.)

We will begin with those two people, the only ones present at that moment in time and then move on to the trial, judgment and punishments.

<u>Adam</u> אָדָם

First there was Adam

The first man, Adam, in the Hebrew אָדָם, is first

mentioned in Genesis 2:7

> *Then the Lord God formed man of dust*
> *from the ground, and breathed into his*
> *nostrils the breath of life; and man*
> *became a living being. (Gen 2:7 NASB)*

Not much is mentioned as a description of the

first man. He was formed from the earth, the dust

thereof. He was therefore an earthly creature. God then

breaths into him the breath of supernatural life and he

becomes a living soul, now having an eternal nature as

well.

Interestingly this can be symbolized as a

combination of a triangle pointing up to heaven overlaid

onto a triangle pointing down to the earth, thus forming what is commonly called the "Star of David". Man, having one foot in the Heavens and the other on the earth. This concept can be seen in the Lord's Prayer: "on earth as it is in heaven".

Eve חַוָּה

Next was Eve or as she was first known "the woman."

> The Lord God fashioned into a woman the rib which He had taken from the man, and brought her to the man. 23 The man said, "This is now bone of my bones, and flesh of my flesh; She shall be called Woman, Because she was taken out of Man. (Gen 2:22 NASB)

The Hebrew word for "the woman" is הָאִשָּׁה (ha eesh-ah) or אִשָּׁה (eesh-ah) for woman.

At first, she is only referred to as "the woman".

Later she is named by Adam and is called "Eve".

And the man called his wife's name Eve;
because she was the mother of all living.
(Gen 3:20 NASB)

The Accused

To summarize, these were the only people present at the fall of mankind, Adam, and Eve.

Adam, the first man was created from the dust of the earth and then through the breath of God a soul was put in him. He was without sin and walked with God. His primary role was to live in the garden and tend to it. Later as a result of his sin, all future mankind inherited death and a death sentence.

The Woman was created by God from Adam's side. She was to be his help mate and partner in the garden. At first, she is simply called "the woman" but later is named "Eve" by Adam. They were to live in the garden together as a couple in perfect harmony.

The two first humans were then to be God's children and people. They would walk with God in the perfect earthly setting of the garden of Eden.

There is not much more which can be said of these two individuals at this point. There is not much written about them anywhere else in the Scriptures. There are other books written about them but they only date to a few hundred years BC and are not part of the Biblical Canon. The writing of Genesis dates to approximately 1500 BC with the events to have taken place 4500-5000 years ago, about 1500 years before the flood.

The Serpent נָחָשׁ

There was one other player present in the garden when this all transpired.

When Eve is tempted in the Bible, the Bible doesn't say "Satan" tempted her but the "serpent". Though we attribute the actions in Genesis 3 to "Satan", that word isn't used, the word used is the word for the "serpent" in Genesis in the original Hebrew is "nachash" נָחָשׁ.

More on this character later.

Other Elements

Here are specific elements and aspects of the case which are pertinent to what took place.

Naked

Genesis states Adam and Eve knew they were naked before they sinned.

> *Now both of them were naked, the man and his wife, <u>and they were not ashamed</u>. (Gen 2:25 TLV emphasis mine)*

Later after what is referred to as "the fall" the reference to their being naked occurs again when they admit to God, they were naked. This happens after the serpent had tempted them into disobedience. Their discovery must be more than realizing they still had no clothing. They were obviously already naked as far as nudity is concerned. That was a foregone conclusion as stated previously. There obviously must be more to this concept.

The Forbidden Fruit

> *but from the tree of the knowledge of good and evil you shall not eat, for in the day that you eat from it you will surely die."*
> *(Gen 2:17 NASB)*

וּמֵעֵץ הַדַּעַת טוֹב וָרָע--לֹא תֹאכַל, מִמֶּנּוּ :כִּי, בְּיוֹם אֲכָלְךָ מִמֶּנּוּ--מוֹת תָּמוּת.

What does the Bible mean when it uses the word "fruit" for the "Fruit of the Tree of the Knowledge of Good and Evil"?

The word for "fruit" throughout the Bible is not only describing something edible but also of something symbolic or analogous for the end results of a decision or action made. It's what results when you consume something or after you make a decision to commit to an action. It can also mean the results of an action.

The term "fruit" generally means the food we are allowed to consume. This may be physical (bread, meat etc.), spiritual (inspirational), or intellectual (Scriptural, experiential).

A physical fruit obviously helps us grow physically; a spiritual fruit helps us grow spiritually and an intellectual fruit helps us grow intellectually. What they did must have gone against all three of these aspects of "fruit" or food. Did they actually eat something?

Motives

God's Motive

The most important motive of all would be God's. What was in God's mind at creation? This is not trying to read God's mind or thoughts of something we don't know, as if it were possible. It's not out of the realm of understanding of what God's intention was if one reads the Bible. It's stated many times over what God wanted to do, what His intentions for mankind were then and still are to this day. God's original motive or plan was a simple and loving one.

God would create a place for Him and His new creature "man(kind)" to dwell together in harmony, in a personal relationship. It's a very simple plan and is well detailed throughout the Bible.

Moreover, I will make My dwelling among you, and My soul will not reject you. (Leviticus 26:11 NASB emphasis mine)

I will be their God and they will be My people. (Jeremiah 31:32 NASB emphasis mine)

The Serpent's Motive

However, the Serpent had a plan of his own. This was to thwart God's plan, deceive the two new people and turn them away from God.

Judgment

God's judgment is real, it is going to happen, and every person will have to face the Eternal Judge and answer for the actions of their lives. This all started in the Garden with the actions of Adam and Eve. God's judgment is not one of vindictive vengeance or retribution, but one of cause and effect.

Closing

To close out and summarize this first short section, we looked at who was present, Adam, Eve, and the Serpent. There was a brief introduction of each of the related elements of the case, naked, fruit, judgment, and motives. The next section will expand on these points and add in more detail as well as what took place.

All the preceding elements will be restated but in much greater detail as the evidence for the crime will begin to be included and laid out point by point. Please continue to keep an open mind until the end. It will become apparent as the evidence builds, there is little doubt as to the veracity of the final conclusion.

Chapter 2 The Case
Introduction

This second section will restate the first section and expand on the various points and their greater implications. There will be some repetition due to the nature of the points being presented.

Some may dismiss these as coincidences. Taken alone any one of the elements which will be presented could be considered a coincidence. When they are all added together the question then becomes, at what point does a substantial number of coincidences begin to tilt or point to a truth? What number of coincidences is needed for something to be true? Is it always just a series of coincidences or do they eventually point to something of significance?

The rest of this book will provide the Biblical proof and evidence to support my contention. Please continue and see how this case builds. As stated previously, those involved are known. The particular elements have been explained. The trial and judgment have taken place. The sentence was imposed and carried out on the Cross or Execution Stake. Now we will see why it all happened the way it did.

After you have read the final conclusion as to what took place, I only ask you to continue reading to see if the amount of evidence compiled is sufficient to make the case. It is not done lightly or as a whim. It has taken a long time to gather the different aspects together to substantiate this thesis. So please do not dismiss it out of hand and wait and see if the arguments make sense or not.

The Details of the Case

So, let's begin, what did Adam and Eve do? How did the Serpent tempt them to do something which caused all of creation to come under a curse?

Provided in the following pages is the evidence.

The Accused Revisited

Adam אָדָם

The first man, Adam, in the Hebrew אָדָם, is first mentioned in Genesis 2:7

> *Then the LORD God formed man of the dust of the ground and breathed into his nostrils the breath of life; and man became a living soul. (Gen 2:7 NASB)*

He was therefore an earthly creature, formed from the earth, the dust thereof. God breaths the breath of supernatural life into him and he becomes a living soul, now having an eternal nature as well.

The word Adam is made up of three Hebrew letters, Aleph, Dalet, and Mem. In Hebrew word pictures this word would by symbolized by

Aleph א symbolizing strength, a leader or the first.

Dalet, ד a door, pathway, to enter.

Mem מ symbolizing water, liquid, massive and chaos.

אָדָם

The word as it stands in a sense means "red man" as related to blood, the Hebrew word for blood being "daam" דָּם which is contained in the word "Adam". It also has a direct connection to "the ground" as with the Hebrew word for "the ground"; "ha adama" הָאֲדָמָה. Thus, we can see "Adam" was taken out of the dust of the ground "ha adama".

With the addition of the sin committed Adam is himself Daam, "blood red". His blood and bloodline then become stained with sin and the only way to wash away that blood stain is through the shedding of blood. He must pay the death penalty. The ground becoming stained with blood as stated with the killing of Able by Cain.

> He said, "What have you done? The voice
> of your brother's blood is crying to Me
> from the ground. (Gen 4:10 NASB)

וַיֹּאמֶר, מֶה עָשִׂיתָ; קוֹל דְּמֵי אָחִיךָ, צֹעֲקִים אֵלַי מִן-
אֲדָמָה

Then we see as Paul states:

Therefore, just as through one-man sin entered into the world, and death through sin, and so death spread to all men, because all sinned (Rom 5:12 NASB)

And so, God covers them in fur, which comes from the death of an animal. This carries greater implications and is the precursor of the sacrificial system which only ends with the actual death of a man. This is all a foreshadow of things to come.

Eve חַוָּה

The Lord God fashioned into a woman the rib which He had taken from the man and brought her to the man. 23 The man said, "This is now bone of my bones, and flesh of my flesh; She shall be called Woman, Because she was taken out of Man. (Gen 2:22 NASB)

The Hebrew word for "the woman" is הָאִשָּׁה (ha eesh-ah) or אִשָּׁה (eesh-ah) for woman.

ה שֶׁ א, the word is made up of the typical three root letters.

In this case Aleph א, Sheen שֶׁ, and Hey ה.

In the word pictures these are Aleph א "strength, leader or first". It's obvious this is "first" as she is the first woman.

The next letter is Sheen שׁ and represents some rather interesting aspects those of "to consume, destroy".

Lastly is the letter Hey הֵ representing a window, to see or reveal. The first one to see or lead to consume or destroy. A question is, what was she the first to see to consume or destroy? She was the first to have interaction with the Serpent who is the one who consumes and destroys. Is it just the serpent in that revelation or was it herself and the hidden nature of humanity?

Later she is actually named by Adam and is called "Eve".

> *Now the man called his wife's name Eve, because she was the mother of all the living. (Gen 3:20 NASB)*

וַיִּקְרָא הָאָדָם שֵׁם אִשְׁתּוֹ, חַוָּה: כִּי הִוא הָיְתָה, אֵם כָּל-חָי

The name Eve is not the accurate pronunciation according to the spelling. This is probably due to the name going through the typical transliteration from the multiple languages the Bible has been translated through. To

pronounce the name Eve from the spelling is as far off the

mark as pronouncing the name Jesus according to the

Hebrew spelling of the true name Yeshua.

The correct pronunciation of the name in Genesis

would be "Ha Va" or "Ha Wah" with a bit of the raspy

sound for the "ha". When the woman was first created

from Adam's rib, she was called eeshah, woman. This

draws on the word for man "eesh" as she was a part of the

man having been created from his rib. After the fall Adam

gives her a name, that of חַוָּה. This means "living" in

Hebrew, from a root that can also mean "snake". A very

interesting connection.

The letters for the name are Chet ח, Vav ו, and Hey

ה.

Chet, "to separate", to "divide" as with fence or an inner room.

Vav, a hook, spike, or nail

Hey, a window, to see, behold.

The name in Hebrew word pictures could come to represent a connection to something that is separate and is revealed. Could the chet represent the inner room analogous of Eve's womb? What is the connection. What is she seeing or revealing? The mother of all living as Adam described her.

Another way to look at it is she revealed the connection. The Vav can reference a connection. This could mean the connection of man to woman in a physical sense? The two, being divided can still be connected. It could also show the connection to the serpent, the one who separates. There is more to Eve as will be explained later.

The Serpent

When Eve is tempted in the Bible, the Bible doesn't say "Satan" tempted her but the "serpent". Though we attribute the actions in Genesis 3 to "Satan", that word isn't used, the original Hebrew word used for the "serpent" is "nachash" נחש.

Nun "life", "action" n נ

Chet, "to separate", "divide" as in a fence ח.

Shin, "devour", "destroy" ש.

What we see is an action designed to separate and devour or destroy. This is a meaning encapsulated in the word for the serpent in Genesis 3 "nachash" נחש. This is precisely what the subtle serpent does. It separates Eve from Adam and both from God, divide and conquer as the saying goes. The serpent devours and destroys the innocent life and relationship they had with God. He thus divides them from God's protective hand.

It is well known serpents and reptiles were once much larger. They did not necessarily all crawl low to the ground at that time. Modern man refers to those creatures by a series of relatively more modern terms like "lizard", "reptile", "dinosaurs", which comes from modern Latin "dinosaurus" from the Greek "Deinos" for "terrible lizard". Even the Bible has different words for the different kinds of reptiles, serpents and lizards. The one in particular in the garden is the word mentioned, the word we translate as "serpent". The issue here is how we today see these words as opposed to the ancients.

In earlier times people weren't quite so scientific, they simply referred to some of these creatures as "dragons". The flying reptiles known as "pterosaurs" can easily be compared to the images of the flying dragons of mythology.

In Genesis 3 we read the following:

But the serpent was shrewder than any animal of the field that Adonai Elohim made. (Gen 3:1 TLV)

This shows the creature being called a "serpent" was similar to the other beasts of the field. It is implied then by the scriptures and interpreted by some that it had the ability to walk on its own. It was a field creature. There still lives what is termed a "dragon" of today known as the Komodo Dragon. This animal fits perfectly the description of the creature in Genesis referred to as "the serpent".

This serpent does walk low to the ground (virtually crawling on its belly) as do all other existing serpents. Some even slither as snakes and legless lizards do today.

This creature, the Komodo Dragon is extremely dangerous and is a voracious eater of virtually anything. It is currently considered the largest of the living reptiles. As mentioned, there are now multiple terms for these creatures. Their specific definitions tend to overlap in their basic descriptions and attributes. They may be called Dinosaurs, Reptiles, Lizards, Dragons and of course Serpents. These are multiple terms for the same basic kinds of creatures.

Consider the known history of the Earth. We have all heard the various periods scientists have devised to try and understand the past such as the "Jurassic" period among others. These along with their different "'ologies", paleontology, zoology and all of those interrelated "'ologies" -theorized what it was like when dinosaur like creatures lived.

The large reptiles of antiquity were dying off. For a number of reasons all happening at the same time they were dwindling. One reason in particular was their size and the subsequent shortage of food required. Food was the key to the Serpent's seduction. The Serpent in the garden coupled the need for food with the desire to be "godlike".

Why did Satan use the form of a serpent to tempt Eve? What was it about the serpent that she later used to tempt Adam? The Serpent was suggesting to Eve through its words and actions a food God had instructed them not to have. A very specific source of food with a very unique quality and ability. The food was the lure or hook with the bait being the promise of becoming "god like".

Satan שׂטן

In Genesis the name or word "Satan" שׂטן, is never used. The passages relating to Adam and Eve in Genesis speak solely of a serpent.

To start we must examine the name or the word we commonly think of as representing "the devil" the word "Satan". The word Satan appears many times throughout the Bible and is used as a verb, noun and adjective. It is never used in the Old Testament to be a proper name of an angel, demon, "devil", or even a person.

The reason is, it is not a name, it's a description. Translated it simply means "adversary or opponent" and all words which stem from this root reflect this attitude or ideology. In the story of Balaam and the donkey, it speaks about THE Angel of the Lord which is also referred to as

"Satan"; since he stood in <u>opposition</u> to the forward motion of Balaam riding his donkey. The term <u>THE</u> Angel of the Lord is believed to represent the pre-incarnate Messiah. In other passages the terms "an angel of the Lord" or "angels of the Lord" are used to represent "rank and file" angels. It is only the phrase THE Angel of the Lord which is understood to represent the pre-incarnate Messiah.

Here are some passages where the word "Satan / שָׂטָן" is used

> *But God was angry because he was going, and the angel of the Lord took his stand in the way as an adversary שָׂטָן (satan) against him. Now he was riding on his donkey and his two servants were with him. (Numbers 22:22 NASB)*

> *The angel of the Lord said to him, "Why have you struck your donkey these three times? Behold, I have come out as an adversary שָׂטָן (satan), because your way was contrary to me. (Numbers 22:32 NASB)*

Then the Lord raised up an adversary to Solomon, Hadad the Edomite; he was of the royal line in Edom. (1Kings 11: 14 NASB)

God also raised up another adversary to him, Rezon the son of Eliada, who had fled from his lord Hadadezer king of Zobah. (1Kings 11:23 NASB.)

And those who repay evil for good, they oppose me שָׂטָן [are my adversaries] (satan), because I follow what is good. (Psalm 38:20 NASB)

But He turned and said to Peter, "Get behind Me, Satan! You are a stumbling block to Me; for you are not setting your mind on God's interests, but man's." (MATTHEW 16:23 NASB)

Yeshua uses the word as He rebukes Peter for opposing His decision. The word takes on a variety of meanings and implications depending on the context.

The context of a Biblical verse is tantamount to any attempt at interpretation. The multiple uses of the word "satan" shows the dangers of taking the Bible superficially or worse. Yeshua was definitely not calling Peter "Satan" as if he was the "devil" in disguise. He was rebuking Peter for standing in opposition to what Yeshua had to do.

"Satan" also seen as the accuser of man, in the feminine form as a noun שטנה (sitna), depicts that aspect in the form of a written accusation. This noun is used only once in the Bible.

> *Now in the reign of Ahasuerus, in the beginning of his reign, they wrote an accusation (sitna) against the inhabitants of Judah and Jerusalem. (Ezra 4:6 NASB emphasis mine)*

Much later during the medieval period the original version of the first letter "shin" letter שׁ (shin) got changed to "sin" שׂ (sin). Which is where we get the current pronunciation of "satan". It's an interesting change considering the implications of the Satan and his relation to the concept of "sin".

Another variant of the word, this time as a verb is "shatan". Interestingly it means to urinate. In the context of the next two verses it can be seen as something more than just a normal bodily function. The action being one of insolence, in essence adversarial.

> *So and more also do God unto the enemies of David, if I leave of all that pertain to him by the morning light any that pisseth against the wall. 1 Samuel 25: 22 KJV*

> *Therefore, behold, I will bring evil upon the house of Jeroboam, and will cut off from Jeroboam him that pisseth against the wall, (1Kings 14:10 KJV.)*

The word is made up of the typical three Hebrew root letters. In this case they are the letters **"Sin"שׁ**;

"Tet" ט and "Nun" ן; to make **"שׁטן"**, this is what

would be read as "sa-taan"; (In the Hebrew it is referred to as "ha sa-taan (the satan) by adding the letter "hey" for "THE" Adversary"). (Remember Hebrew reads right to left). השׂטן

The Shin שׁ again represents teeth, to devour or destroy.

The Tet ט is like a snake which surrounds,

The Nun ן has the word picture of a fish or new sprout of vegetation. It can symbolize action or life.

As stated, the letter nun is often placed after a root to create a phrase that isolates or personifies the conceptual action of the root.

The "nun" then creates the rest of the phrase, in this case "satan" is "that which surrounds and devours" something. The name or word "satan" contains the essence of that which surrounds and devours life.

Next, we see that the letter "nun" also has an even more specific meaning which emphasizes the point being made. The letter "nun" can be seen in the word "neen" נין which is made up of Nun, Yud, Nun. It can be found in Genesis 12:23 and Job 18:19 and references an offspring or son. "Satan" could then through Hebrew word pictures have the essential concept of "That which surrounds and devours the son or offspring".

Consider the word for son "ben". In Hebrew word pictures it means "*the life of the family*". So "satan" as a word is essentially that which (or who) surrounds and devours "*the son / life of the family*". According to Dr.Frank Seekins in his book "Hebrew Word Pictures", the word for son "ben" comes from the word "bana" meaning "to build".

Destroying or devouring the "son" in this case would be the complete opposite of building, it would literally be destroying. Consider the implications of destroying at the time of Creation. This action by the Adversary would be directly against God who had just created all there is. He would be attempting to destroy Creation.

Satan is as we know, in direct opposition to the Son of God. He truly seeks to destroy Him. Did not "Satan" do that in the Garden? His efforts destroyed the potential future life of the family as well as creation itself?

There are many who attribute a variety of specific names to this identity of the Adversary. Most of them refer to other gods of ancient cultures and not so much the chief of the fallen angels. If someone really wants this character to have a specific name, they can look to the non-canonical book of Enoch. The same book referenced in the Biblical book of Jude.

> [1]*Enoch 6:2 And the angels, the children of the heaven, saw and lusted after them, and said to one another: 'Come, let us choose us wives from among the children of men and beget us children 3. And **Semjâzâ,** who was their leader, said unto them: 'I fear you will not indeed agree to do this deed, and I alone shall have to pay the penalty of a great sin.'.*

So how did the two terms become synonymous and how does it become the so called "Devil"?

---

[1] *Presented ONLY as a point of interest and has no bearing on this discourse or as attributing the name used as that being of the Adversary / Satan. This must be made perfectly clear.*

The Connection

In Isaiah 14 it states a famous passage interpreted as referencing the fallen angel known as "satan", though it does not use the word. The phrasing goes like this:

> *How you have fallen from heaven, O Brightstar, son of the dawn! How you are cut down to the earth, you who made the nations prostrate! (Isaiah 14:12 TLV)*

(Remember, right to left!)

אֵיךְ נָפַלְתָּ מִשָּׁמַיִם, הֵילֵל בֶּן-שָׁחַר; נִגְדַּעְתָּ לָאָרֶץ,
חוֹלֵשׁ עַל-גּוֹיִם.

In this passage it refers to "day -star, son of the morning"; הֵילֵל בֶּן-שָׁחַר, Helel Ben Shahar. It was what was commonly thought of as the morning star also known as the planet Venus. An ancient word for the planet Venus is "Lucifer". That is how the name got attached to the Biblical Adversary "the satan". It's not a Biblical name, nor is it a name of an angel, spirit or any other kind of entity. It's not even a Hebrew or Aramaic word.

The word itself is from the old English term Lucifer which comes from the Latin Lux or Luc and references the "morning star" or Venus in the morning sky before sunrise,"

The name of the planet was injected into the Bible due to the morning star reference. However, it is not in the original Hebrew text. The Adversary is very good at deceiving and confusing people, this is one simple example. Lucifer is just the ancient name of the planet Venus and nothing more.

In the book of Revelation another very interesting word is used, "dragon". This word has different nuances to it. Before people used the word "dinosaur" for the ancient giant reptiles and "serpents", the word or term used was "dragon".

The word "dragon," according to the Oxford English Dictionary (1966), comes from an Old French word which itself comes from the Latin word for serpent "dracon". Supposedly this came from an ancient Greek word "Spakov", also meaning "serpent".

In some ancient cultures' dragons had the ability to speak. So-called "modern man" views "dragons" as mythical, so there is an inherent hesitation to use this word. In reality it was just an ancient term for what we today would call "dinosaurs". Modern man is so much more "scientific" now, thinking we are so much smarter than the ancients.

It is in the book of the Revelation to John where the direct connection of the Adversary / Satan is made with the Serpent in Eden.

> *And war broke out in heaven, Michael and his angels making war against the dragon. The dragon and his angels fought, 8 but they were not strong enough, and there was no longer any place for them in heaven. 9 And the great dragon was thrown down—the ancient serpent, called the devil and satan, who deceives the whole world. He was thrown down to the earth, and his angels were thrown down with him. (Rev 12: 7 TLV emphasis mine)*

> *He seized the dragon—the ancient serpent, who is the devil and satan (Rev 20:2 TLV)*

So now there is a direct correlation between "Satan" and the (ancient) "serpent". This is the proof the serpent in Eden is ha satan, the Adversary.

Eden is where the serpent became the opponent of God, becoming the "satan". Before that moment in time it was just another creature, all be it a smart one, another beast of the field as in Genesis 3.

A serpent did not beguile Eve, it was "satan" in the form of a serpent who tricked or beguiled Eve who then passed the temptation on to Adam.

Regardless of a specific name, the serpent of Eden is the Adversary, the one commonly referred to as "the devil". His goal as discussed was and is to destroy God's creation, "man" and to set himself up on the throne of God.

The Forbidden Fruit

A lot of this rests on the understanding of what that fruit was. What kind of tree was it? Let's examine again the "Fruit of the Tree of the Knowledge of Good and Evil". The tree at the "root" of all this. Restating what was said earlier:

> *But of the Tree of the Knowledge of Good and Evil you must not eat. For when you eat from it, you most assuredly will die!' (Gen 2:17 TLV)*

וּמֵעֵץ, הַדַּעַת טוֹב וָרָע--לֹא תֹאכַל, מִמֶּנּוּ: כִּי, בְּיוֹם אֲכָלְךָ מִמֶּנּוּ--מוֹת תָּמוּת

What does the Bible mean when it uses the word "fruit" for the "Fruit of the Tree of the Knowledge of Good and Evil"?

As the ancient sages and Rabbis up to today teach, there is a process of Biblical interpretation which includes something called "remez". This is where one matches a word from one verse to the same word in other locations as a means to form a larger understanding of the passages, subject and word itself.

The word "fruit" throughout the Bible is not only describing something edible but also of something symbolic or analogous for the end results of a decision, or action made. It's what results when you consume something or after you make a decision to commit to an action. It can mean what is produced from something other than a just a tree of some kind.

The term "fruit" also obviously means the food we are allowed to consume. That which comes from a fruit bearing tree. However, it may also refer to generic physical food for our body such as bread, meat and so on. It can also be spiritual food, that which helps our spirit, is inspirational, such as Scriptures, songs, words of wisdom or advice. It can be intellectual food, "food for thought" which would come from other sources like personal experience, books and teachings from someone else. A good question is, did they actually eat something?

The Hebrew word for fruit is **"p'ri"** פְּרִי

The word (p'ri) is used in Genesis for the fruit of "the tree of the knowledge of good and evil". etz ha da'at tov va ra

> *but from the fruit of the tree which is in the middle of the garden, God has said, 'You shall not eat from it or touch it, or you will die.'" (Gen 3:3 NASB)*

This Hebrew word is used extensively throughout the Bible. We find it referencing a wide variety of things. It first appears in Genesis:

> *with the "Fruit tree, yielding fruit after his kind", (Genesis 1:11 NASB)*

but from the fruit of the tree which is in the middle of the garden, God has said, 'You shall not eat from it or touch it, or you will die.'" (Gen 3:3 NASB the verse in question)

Cain brought of the fruit of the earth", (Gen 4:3NASB.)

"Am I in the place of God, who has withheld from you the fruit of the womb?", (Genesis 30:2 NASB)

We can see these phrases used repeated throughout the Bible, "fruit bearing tree", "fruit of the womb", "fruit of the land", "fruit of the earth". In Deuteronomy 28:4 we see similar metaphors with "**fruit** of your body, **fruit** of your land,", "**fruit** of your cattle", "**fruit** of your doings", "**fruit** of lies" and the list goes on.

The point is, what is really meant by the term "fruit" of the tree of the knowledge of good and evil (etz ha da'at tov va ra)? What is the biblical concept of what a "fruit" is within this context and how does it relate to what Eve and then Adam did?

The word for Fruit in the Bible is "p'ri" (prounounced "peh-ree" or "p'ree") and is made up of three letters, reading right to left "peh", "resh", "yud". פְּ רִ י. The word pictures are:

Peh, פְּ to speak, mouth, to open.

Resh, ר the head the highest and the head of a man, and the

Yud י a hand, to work, a deed or to make.

There are many variants which can be made from these clues. The action of speaking to open the head of a person as in revealing knowledge. To make open the head or mind of a man for the gaining of knowledge or wisdom. It is a common understanding within Rabbinic teaching the

Yud can represent or imply the Messiah in a variety of words.

An interesting verse again likens children and descendents to fruit as in Psalm 21.

> *"Their fruit shall you destroy from the earth, and their seed from among the children of men" (Psalm 21:10 KJV.)*

Another analogy is found in Psalm 92.

> *" they shall still bring forth fruit in old age." (Psalm 92:14 KJV)*

There we see it used as what a person accomplishes.

Here it refers to what God has accomplished with Creation.

> *"Who water the mountains from Your upper chambers; the earth is full of the fruit of Your works." (Psalm 104:13 TLV.)*

In Proverbs the word "fruit" is used to characterize what a person does:

> *" The fruit of the righteous is a tree of life, and whoever wins souls is wise." (Prov 11:30 TLV.)*

In this next verse it takes on a similar reference to the results of what someone does or more to the point "says":

> *" From the fruit of his mouth a man's stomach is filled—with the harvest of his lips he is satisfied.". 21:" Death and life are in the control of the tongue. Those who indulge in it will eat its fruit.." (Prov 18:20 TLV)*

> *" She considers a field and buys it. From the fruit of her hands she plants a vineyard. (Prov 31:16 TLV)*

These metaphors are numerous, "fruit of the land, womb, tree, lips, tongue, labors, field, tree, vine. In the New Testament we see it is again used to refer to what someone does as in *"you shall know them by their fruits"*.

It is clear the word or term "fruit" (**p'ri**) means more than just a piece of edible vegetation. The analogy of Adam and Eve eating an apple is absurd on its face as most realize. It's also not of their having "premarital sex" as many had thought throughout the centuries. Adam had not "known" Eve until after this all happened; after God removed them out of the land, the Garden of Eden.

Using the first and second methods of interpretation, the parshat (the written word as it stands) and the remez (clues contained in the written word and books), we can see if the word "fruit" is used in a context which could point to what took place. By using this common and ancient Jewish form of interpretation these theological and theoretical references to what happened in Eden can then be easily supported.

Presented here are passages which are directly on point to this discussion. The word for fruit as it appears in Genesis (as stated is p'ri) and appears in numerous places throughout the Tanak (Old Testament). Some of these passages are on point to what is being presented.

> *The woman said to the serpent, "From the fruit of the trees of the garden we may eat; 3 but from the fruit of the tree which is in the middle of the garden, God has said, 'You shall not eat from it or touch it, or you will die.'" (Gen 3:2 NASB)*

> *When the woman saw that the tree was good for food, and that it was a delight to the eyes, and that the tree was desirable to make one wise, she took from its fruit and ate; and she gave also to her husband with her, and he ate. (Gen 3:6 NASB)*

> *Then Jacob's anger burned against Rachel, and he said, "Am I in the place of God, who has withheld from you the fruit of the womb?" (Gen 30:2 NASB)*

> *He will love you and bless you and multiply you; He will also bless the fruit of*

your womb and the fruit of your ground,
your grain and your new wine and your
oil, the increase of your herd and the
young of your flock, in the land which He
swore to your forefathers to give you.
(Deut 7:13 NASB)

Here is a great example of how the text uses the word for "fruit", "p'ri" to reference something which is not a plant or related to one. Two translations are used to show how the words appears and is used in the text.

Baruch shall be the pri of thy womb, and
the pri of thy adamah, and the pri of thy
animals, the increase of thy livestock, and
the flocks of thy sheep. (Deut 28:4 OJB)

Blessed shall be the offspring of your body
and the produce of your ground and the
offspring of your beasts, the increase of
your herd and the young of your flock.
(Deut 28:4 NASB)

Again, the same motif.

And Hashem shall make thee plenteous in
goods, in the pri of thy womb, and in the
pri of thy livestock, and in the pri of thy

ground, in ha'adamah which Hashem swore unto Avotecha to give thee. (Deut 28:11 OJB)

The Lord will make you abound in prosperity, in the offspring of your body and in the offspring of your beast and in the produce of your ground, in the land which the Lord swore to your fathers to give you. (Deut 28:11 NASB)

Fruit was not always shown as a blessing but was also used as a curse depending on the situation.

Arur shall be the <u>pri</u> of thy womb, and the <u>pri</u> of thy adamah, the increase of thy livestock, and the flocks of thy sheep. (Deut 28:18 OJB)

Cursed shall be the offspring of your body and the produce of your ground, the increase of your herd and the young of your flock. (Deut 28:18 NASB)

In this next verse in the Torah there is an actual direct reference to eating one's young at time of strife.

You will eat the fruit of your womb, the flesh of your sons and daughters Adonai your God has given you, in the siege and stress with which your enemies will distress you. 54 The most tender and delicate man among you—his eye will become evil against his brother and the wife of his bosom and the rest of his children that he has left. 55 He will not give to a single one of them from his children's flesh that he will eat, because nothing else is left for him in the siege and stress with which your enemy will distress you within all your town gates. 56 The tender and delicate woman among you, who never ventured to set the sole of her foot on the ground out of delicateness and tenderness—her eye will become evil against the husband of her bosom and her son and daughter. 57 For in secret she will eat her afterbirth that issues from between her legs and the children she bears, for lack of anything else in the siege and stress with which your enemy will distress you within all your gates. (Deut 28:53 TLV)

Then the Lord your God will prosper you abundantly in all the work of your hand, in the offspring of your body and in the offspring of your cattle and in the produce of your ground, for the Lord will again rejoice over you for good, just as He rejoiced over your fathers; (Deut 30:9 NASB)

Behold, children are a heritage of Adonai —the fruit of the womb is a reward. (Psalm 127:3 TLV)

The Lord has sworn to David a truth from which He will not turn back: "Of the fruit of your body I will set upon your throne. (Psalm 132:11 NASB)

Again, it is demonstrated the word "fruit" (Heb.

"p'ri") is used for more than just a piece of edible

vegetation and represents that which is produced by

someone or something. Over and over it's the same word

used in Genesis to also represent the so-called "forbidden

fruit". The list of other passages which contain this doesn't

end there.

The First Fruits

Then the Lord spoke to Moses, saying, 10 "Speak to the sons of Israel and say to them, 'When you enter the land which I am going to give to you and reap its harvest, then you shall bring in the sheaf of the first fruits of your harvest to the priest. Leviticus 23:9 NASB

This term "first fruits" is an interesting one and helps to make the connection being presented. We see it used as the "first fruits" of the harvest, of the womb, of the land, of the herds and flocks. In the next couple of passages, we see it used specifically to describe Yeshua.

But now is Messiah risen from the dead, [and] become the first fruits of them that slept. (1Corinthians 15:20 TLV)

But every man in his own order: Messiah the first fruits; afterward they that are Messiah's at his coming. (1Corinthians 15:23 TLV)

The first part "The Fruit of the Tree", has been shown to be a metaphor, it's not food but something which comes from or is produced from that tree.

The fruit of that tree is knowledge and that which results from it. Many will say this is the knowledge of disobedience, in part this is true. However, there is more to the description of the tree. It is not just a tree of knowledge but "The Tree of the Knowledge of Good and Evil". This is the key to this mystery and once understood the beginning of wisdom.

Naked

Genesis states Adam and Eve knew they were naked before they sinned. Later after what is referred to as "the fall" this occurs again when they admit to God they were naked; after the serpent had tempted them into disobedience. Their discovery must be more than realizing they had no clothing. They were obviously already naked as far as nudity is concerned and were aware of it. Look at the passage where they already know they are "naked". It shows that was a foregone conclusion.

> *Now both of them were naked, the man and his wife, and they were not ashamed.* *(Gen 2:25 TLV)*

The root word for "naked" in Genesis is "ee-roome" here spelled "ah-room-meem" עֲרוּמִּים since it is in its plural form as they were both naked and refers to their being nude, without clothing. It wasn't until afterwards, after they sinned they began stitching leaves together to make clothing.

There must be more to the word or concept of "naked" than just nudity in this setting and circumstance.

Take a look at the word "naked" and its implications. Here are some synonyms for the word and concept of "naked": barren, defenseless, divested, exposed, helpless, leafless, open, unconcealed, uncovered, unprotected, unveiled, vulnerable. Note their relationship to the concept of being without protection. When one is naked, one can be exposed to any number of things.

Prior to the fall they were naked only so far as being without clothing. Up until that point they were walking with God. Now they had become corrupted and their closeness to God and the protection they incurred from that closeness was breached. Adam and Eve were not only naked physically as they had already been, but they had also become exposed spiritually.

There was then a clear way in by the Adversary. They were "exposed" to future temptations and sin. More importantly, they were then vulnerable to the wrath and punishment of God. They were naked, "exposed" before God's judgment and the retribution for their disobedience. No longer were they pure, they (and mankind) were from then on "uncovered".

Listed here are just some of the places we find variants for the word "naked" in the Scriptures. It's easily seen how many relate to the point being made, Adam and Eve did not suddenly discover they were "nude" / 'without clothing" but were now vulnerable to the Wrath of God. They had become unprotected and had moved away from the protection of God by their sin.

*And they were both naked, the man and his
wife, and <u>were not ashamed</u>. (Gen 2:25
TLV)*

So, restated they knew already they were nude as

one of the definitions of "naked". At this point in time they

were still under the protection of God. They were still

spiritually covered, and their nudity was a sign of their

innocence. Most importantly, they knew already of their

being naked, "nude" in the obvious sense. However, at the

beginning of the next chapter Gen 3, the serpent enters the

scenario. The Bible translates as:

*Now the serpent was more crafty than any
beast of the field which the Lord God had
made. And he said to the woman, "Indeed,
has God said, 'You shall not eat from any
tree of the garden'?". (Gen 3:1 NASB)*

וְהַנָּחָשׁ הָיָה עָרוּם

The Hebrew word used for "subtle" in this place is "

עָרוּם, "Ah-room", and is a variant of the same root word

for "naked". It represents the uncovering, their exposure. The serpent tricked them into becoming "uncovered" or "naked". But in what sense of the term?

What was it the serpent was uncovering? They were already naked or nude, without clothing. What the serpent did was to cause them to remove their innocence and the covering of God's protection. That was the protection from God's righteous judgment due to their innocence. Since they had disobeyed God they were uncovered, unprotected and open to God's judgment and punishment.

> *Then the eyes of both of them were opened, and they knew that they were naked; and they sewed fig leaves together and made themselves loin coverings. (Gen 3:7 NASB)*

Now they know they are unprotected. They are "naked" before God's judgment. They already knew they were without clothing, that was seen in Gen 2:25. This repeating of the point they were naked must then refer to another aspect of the concept of being naked. They were then unprotected, without God's spiritual covering.

> *And He said, "Who told you that you were naked? Have you eaten from the tree of which I commanded you not to eat?" (Gen 3:11 NASB)*

This emphasizes the point of their realization, they had sinned and lost that closeness with God. They were afraid of His anger and wrath. They were not afraid before. They were now "exposed" to judgment and any subsequent punishment. They had become afraid of God.

> *And He said, "Who told you that you were naked? (Gen 3:11 NASB)*

Adam answers by avoiding the question.

> *The man said, "The woman whom You gave to be with me, she gave me from the tree, and I ate." (Gen 3: 12 NASB)*

All he does is state what basically took place and

tries to shift the blame. The answer is, no one actually told

them they were naked, they realized it on their own. They

knew what they had done was obviously wrong and were

ashamed of their actions. They realized they were guilty

and had no protection from God's wrath. Whatever it was

they did, it was blatantly obvious it was wrong. Far more

than just "eating a piece of fruit". Far more than just being

"nude" and ashamed of it.

Here is an assortment of passages all containing the

idea of being naked.

> *And when Moses saw that the people were*
> *naked (for Aaron had made them naked*
> *unto their shame among their enemies)*
> *(Exo 32:25 KJ21)*

Many commentaries agree the word "naked" is the

best translation for the Hebrew word in this passage as the

Israelites were dancing about in a licentious frenzy. Their

actions and sinfulness became exposed, "naked for all to see".

As we see, God's judgment then comes down upon them and three thousand were killed. They had become naked, not only physically but spiritually as well, hence the imposition of God's judgment. They like Adam and Eve had become naked, unprotected from God's wrath and judgment.

> *For the LORD brought Judah low because of Ahaz king of Israel; for he made Judah naked, and transgressed sore against the LORD. (2Ch 28:19 KJ21)*

This passage tells of how Ahaz had corrupted Judah and thus they were naked (exposed and unprotected) before God's judgment. It references the land of Judah and not an individual. Is it suggesting the entire land of Judah then threw off their clothes and were all naked? Of course not. It is clear it is pointing to a situation where Judah was unprotected and open to God's wrath. This is the main point, that of being "naked" is not limited to being without clothing.

> They cause the naked to lodge without clothing, that they have no covering in the cold. (Job 24:7 KJ21)

Here the nakedness is both nudity as well as unprotected, in this case against the natural elements. Clothing is a protection from the elements as we know. This reinforces the concept of being naked is being unprotected.

> Hell is naked before him, and destruction hath no covering. (Job 26:6 KJ21)

Here the word for "hell" is actually "sheol" for grave or pit. But how can a pit be "naked" as in no clothing? Again, it is showing the concept of being naked is not limited to clothing.

Neither is there any creature that is not manifest in his sight: but all things are naked and opened unto the eyes of him with whom we have to do. (Heb 4:13 KJ21)

Because thou say, I am rich, and increased with goods, and have need of nothing; and know not that thou art wretched, and miserable, and poor, and blind, and naked: (Rev 3:17 KJ21)

Behold, I come as a thief. Blessed is he that watch, and keep his garments, lest he walk naked and they see his shame. (Rev 16:15 KJ21)

And the ten horns which thou saw upon the beast, these shall hate the whore, and shall make her desolate and naked, and shall eat her flesh, and burn her with fire. (Rev 17:16 KJ21)

All of these passages and many more show the term for "naked" is not limited to simply wearing no clothes. The passages show a clear line of thought of naked as meaning to be exposed or unprotected. In some cases, directly on point of being exposed spiritually to God's judgment.

The Serpent tempted Eve and thus Adam into exposing themselves to God's judgment.

> *But the serpent was shrewder than any animal of the field that Adonai Elohim made. So it said to the woman, "Did God really say, 'You must not eat from all the trees of the garden'?" 2 The woman said to the serpent, "Of the fruit of the trees, we may eat. 3 But of the fruit of the tree which is in the middle of the garden, God said, 'You must not eat of it and you must not touch it, or you will die.'" 4 The serpent said to the woman, "You most assuredly won't die! 5 For God knows that when you eat of it, your eyes will be opened, and you will be like God, knowing good and evil." 6 Now the woman saw that the tree was good for food, and that it was a thing of lust for the eyes, and that the tree was desirable for imparting wisdom. So, she took of its fruit and she ate. She also gave to her husband who was with her and he ate. (Gen 3:1 TLV)*

Now they knew they had sinned and were exposed to judgment.

> Then the eyes of both of them were opened and they knew that they were naked; so they sewed fig leaves together and made for themselves loin-coverings. 8 And they heard the sound of Adonai Elohim going to and fro in the garden in the wind of the day. So the man and his wife hid themselves from the presence of Adonai Elohim in the midst of the Tree of the garden. 9 Then Adonai Elohim called to the man and He said to him, "Where are you?" 10 Then he said, "Your sound—I heard it in the garden and I was afraid. Because I am naked, I hid myself." (Gen 3:7 TLV)

Adam and Eve were now exposed to God's judgment and retribution. They knew it. What they had done was blatantly obvious to them. Their sin was self-evident. Just biting into a piece of fruit would not do that. Whatever it was they did was far more obvious.

Chapter 3 Plans are set in motion

God's plan:

God would create a place for Him and His new creature "man(kind)" to dwell together in harmony, in a personal relationship. It's a very simple plan and is well detailed throughout the Bible.

> *"I will dwell among the sons of Israel and will be their God. (Ex 29:45 NASB)*

> *"They shall know that I am the LORD their God who brought them out of the land of Egypt, that I might dwell among them; I am the LORD their God. (Ex 29:46 NASB)*

> *Moreover, I will make My dwelling among you, and My soul will not reject you. (Leviticus 26:11 NASB)*

> *"You shall send away both male and female; you shall send them outside the camp so that they will not defile their camp where I dwell in their midst." (Numbers 5:3 NASB)*

'You shall not defile the land in which you live, in the midst of which I dwell; for I the LORD am dwelling in the midst of the sons of Israel.'" (Numbers 35:34 NASB)

"I will dwell among the sons of Israel and will not forsake My people Israel." (1Kings 6:13 NASB)

Then I will give them a heart to know Me—for I am Adonai—and they will be My people, and I will be their God. (Jeremiah 24:7 NASB)

I will be their God and they will be My people. (Jeremiah 31:32 NASB)

Then they will be My people and I will be their God. (Ezekiel 37:23 NASB)

"My dwelling place also will be with them; and I will be their God, and they will be My people. (Ezekiel 37:27 NASB)

He said to me, "Son of man, this is the place of My throne and the place of the soles of My feet, where I will dwell among the sons of Israel forever And the house of Israel will not again defile My holy name, neither they nor their kings, by their harlotry and by the corpses of their kings when they die, (Ezekiel 43:7 NASB)

"Now let them put away their harlotry and the corpses of their kings far from Me; and I will dwell among them forever. (Ezekiel 43:9 NASB)

"Sing for joy and be glad, O daughter of Zion; for behold I am coming and I will dwell in your midst," declares the LORD. (Zechariah 2:10 NASB)

"Many nations will join themselves to the LORD in that day and will become My people Then I will dwell in your midst, and you will know that the LORD of hosts has sent Me to you. (Zechariah 2:11 NASB)

And the Word became flesh, and dwelt among us, and we saw His glory, glory as of the only begotten from the Father, full of grace and truth. (John 1:14 NASB emphasis mine)

just as God said, "I will dwell in them and walk among them; and I will be their God, and they shall be My people. (2Cor 6:16 NASB emphasis mine)

And I will be their God, and they shall be My people. (Hebrews 8:10 NASB)

And I heard a loud voice from the throne, saying, "Behold, the tabernacle of God is among men, and He will dwell among them, and they shall be His people, and God Himself will be among them, (Revelation 21:3 NASB)

It is clear, time and time again God states categorically His desire is to dwell with man.

The process is just as simple. God would enter the world as a man, the Messiah and dwell with man. He would do this through the woman Eve before she has any physical relationship with her eventual husband Adam. As the Scriptures point out, He would be born through a virgin. Yes, it says Eve, it is not a typographical error. This was the plan in Eden. God would be with man, Immanuel; God with us. This is the crux of the matter. From here on the evidence will build exponentially to prove this and establish what took place.

Satan's Plan

However, Satan had a plan of his own. Satan always wanted to raise himself up to the throne of God.

> How you have fallen from heaven, O Brightstar, son of the dawn! How you are cut down to the earth, you who made the nations prostrate! 13 You said in your heart: "I will ascend to heaven, I will exalt my throne above the stars of God. I will sit upon the mount of meeting, in the uttermost parts of the north. 14 I will ascend above the high places of the clouds—I will make myself like Elyon." (Isaiah 14:12 TLV)

Satan's plan stands in stark contrast to God's plan. Satan was jealous of God's new favorite creature, "man". Satan also did not like the idea of God becoming one of these creatures who would then rule over him. So, he sets his own plan in motion, to destroy this new creature.

Satan would use the soon to be parents of the child to do the deed for several reasons.

1. Satan's plan is a direct manipulation and corruption of God's new favorite creature "man". This plan if successful would cause man to become sinful, lose God's protection and become subject to God's judgment.

2. The plan causes the new creature to destroy itself at the same time destroying one part of God's Triune nature, the visible, physical "Son" of God.

3. Their actions would be a capital crime requiring the death penalty under God's righteous nature and judgment. Not only does he destroy this aspect of God's Nature, but mankind itself right at the onset of its existence before it can grow and multiply. And most evil of all, God would have to carry out the execution of the new creation.

4. Satan would appear as a serpent and play on the

   naiveté of Eve.

So, Satan put his plan in motion. With the addition of what took place, the simplicity of the plan is obvious. The plan ostensibly worked, but only to a degree. God cannot be outsmarted even by an angel. More elements of his plan will show up later.

The fact of the Judgment

A final judgment is at the core of Judeo-Christian theology. It is inevitable; we cannot avoid facing His Throne. The Old Testament definitely speaks of a final judgment and of being judged. Some of the books and personages from the Old Testament and Biblical history which discuss or refer to the final judgment include David, Isaiah and Daniel. Here are examples from the New Covenant / Testament and is a list of quotes beginning with the book of Jude.

> *It was also about these men that Enoch, in the seventh generation from Adam, prophesied, saying, "Behold, the Lord came with many thousands of His holy ones, 15 to execute judgment upon all, and to convict all the ungodly of all their ungodly deeds which they have done in an ungodly way, and of all the harsh things*

which ungodly sinners have spoken against Him." (Jude 1:14 NASB)

That is a reference to a quote from the book of Enoch.

9. And behold! He cometh with ten thousands of [His] holy ones <u>to execute judgment</u> upon all, and to destroy [all] the ungodly: and to convict all flesh of all the works [of their ungodliness] which they have ungodly committed, and of all the hard things which ungodly sinners [have spoken] against Him.."

(https://www.sacred-texts.com/bib/boe/boe004.htm)

The book of Psalms, Isaiah and Daniel also speaks of the Lord's final judgment of humanity.

But the Lord abides forever; He has established His throne for judgment, 8 And He will judge the world in righteousness; He will execute judgment for the peoples with equity. 9 The Lord also will be a stronghold for the oppressed, (Psalm 9:7 NASB)

And He will judge between the nations, and will render decisions for many peoples; (Isaiah 2:4 NASB)

And He will judge between many peoples and render decisions for mighty, distant nations. (Micah 4:3 NASB)

Daniel 12-2 2 Many of those who sleep in the dust of the ground will awake, these to everlasting life, but the others to disgrace and everlasting contempt. NASB

For God will bring every act to judgment, everything which is hidden, whether it is good or evil. (Ecclesiastes 12:14 NASB)

Moses, the one called "The Law Giver" would receive commands, advice and direction from God personally. This included how to judge the people. Moses comments on his being the overall judge of the Israelites.

It came about the next day that Moses sat to judge the people, and the people stood about Moses from the morning until the evening. (Exodus 18:13 NASB)

Here Moses continues as he explains his role as the judge of the Israelites;

> *When they have a dispute, it comes to me, and I judge between a man and his neighbor and make known the statutes of God and His laws." (Ex. 18-16 NASB)*

This is the same tone regarding judgment as is in the book of Enoch.

> *Enoch 9:3 "And now to you, the holy ones of heaven, the souls of men make their suit, saying, "Bring our cause before the Most High."'*

https://www.sacred-texts.com/bib/boe/boe012.htm

Just as Moses says the Israelites came to him for justice and judgment; Enoch tells of mankind seeking justice, and the desire to plead their case before the Great Judge of all, God.

Judgment in the New Testament

The proof of a judgment is seen in the New Testament with the following passages:

> All the nations will be gathered before Him; and He will separate them from one another, as the shepherd separates the sheep from the goats; 33 and He will put the sheep on His right, and the goats on the left. (Matthew 25:32 NASB)

> dealing out retribution to those who do not know God and to those who do not obey the gospel of our Lord Jesus. 9 These will pay the penalty of eternal destruction, away from the presence of the Lord and from the glory of His power, (2Thessalonians 1:8 NASB)

> and if He condemned the cities of Sodom and Gomorrah to destruction by reducing them to ashes, having made them an example to those who would live ungodly lives thereafter; 7 and if He rescued righteous Lot, oppressed by the sensual conduct of unprincipled men 8 (for by

what he saw and heard that righteous man, while living among them, felt his righteous soul tormented day after day by their lawless deeds), 9 then the Lord knows how to rescue the godly from temptation, and to keep the unrighteous under punishment for the day of judgment, (2Peter 2:6 NASB)

Finally

Then I saw thrones, and they sat on them, and judgment was given to them. (Revelation 20:4 NASB)

God's judgment is real, it is going to happen, and every person will have to face the Eternal Judge and answer for the actions of their lives. This all started in the Garden with the actions of Adam, Eve and the Serpent with God's judgment over them.

God's judgment is not one of vindictive vengeance or retribution, but one of cause and effect. If God was not a loving and forgiving God, the way of escaping this judgment would have never been provided. God would have just allowed people to do what they did, and if they failed, they "got what they deserved". But God is a loving and forgiving God and sent His only Son to take our place and take upon Himself the punishment humanity has earned individually as well as collectively. The sentence of death first handed down in Eden.

> *Who has believed our message? And to whom has the arm of the Lord been revealed? 2 For He grew up before Him like a tender shoot, And like a root out of parched ground; He has no stately form or majesty That we should look upon Him, Nor appearance that we should be attracted to Him. 3 He was despised and forsaken of men, A man of sorrows and acquainted with grief; And like one from whom men hide their face He was despised, and we did not esteem Him. 4 Surely our griefs He Himself bore, And our sorrows He carried; Yet we ourselves esteemed Him stricken, Smitten of God, and afflicted. 5 But He was pierced*

through for our transgressions, He was crushed for our iniquities; The chastening for our well-being fell upon Him, And by His scourging we are healed. 6 All of us like sheep have gone astray, each of us has turned to his own way; But the Lord has caused the iniquity of us all To fall on Him. 7 He was oppressed, and He was afflicted, Yet He did not open His mouth; Like a lamb that is led to slaughter, And like a sheep that is silent before its shearers, So, He did not open His mouth. 8 By oppression and judgment He was taken away; And as for His generation, who considered That He was cut off out of the land of the living for the transgression of my people, to whom the stroke was due? 9 His grave was assigned with wicked men, Yet He was with a rich man in His death, Because He had done no violence, Nor was there any deceit in His mouth. 10 But the Lord was pleased to crush Him, putting Him to grief; If He would render Himself as a guilt offering, He will see His offspring, He will prolong His days, And the good pleasure of the Lord will prosper in His hand. 11 As a result of the anguish of His soul, He will see it and be satisfied; By His knowledge, the Righteous One, My

Servant, will justify the many, As He will bear their iniquities. 12 Therefore, I will allot Him a portion with the great, And He will divide the booty with the strong; Because He poured out Himself to death and was numbered with the transgressors; Yet He Himself bore the sin of many, and interceded for the transgressors. (Isaiah 53:1 NASB)

God proved His righteousness and righteous judgment by submitting His own son to it.

A Righteous Judge

Scriptures demonstrate the Lord's Righteousness and Justice. This concept is exemplified by a number of actions by the Creator. There is the imposition of righteous laws and demands as in Exodus 20.

"I am the Lord your God, who brought you out of the land of Egypt, out of the house of slavery.

3 "You shall have no other gods before Me.

4 "You shall not make for yourself an idol, or any likeness of what is in heaven above or on the earth beneath or in the water under the earth. 5 You shall not worship them or serve them; for I, the Lord your God, am a jealous God, visiting the iniquity of the fathers on the children, on the third and the fourth generations of those who hate Me, 6 but showing lovingkindness to thousands, to those who love Me and keep My commandments.

7 "You shall not take the name of the Lord your God in vain, for the Lord will not leave him unpunished who takes His name in vain.

8 "Remember the sabbath day, to keep it holy. 9 Six days you shall labor and do all your work, 10 but the seventh day is a sabbath of the Lord your God; in it you shall not do any work, you or your son or your daughter, your male or your female servant or your cattle or your sojourner who stays with you. 11 For in six days the Lord made the heavens and the earth, the sea and all that is in them, and rested on the seventh day; therefore the Lord blessed the sabbath day and made it holy.

12 "Honor your father and your mother, that your days may be prolonged in the land which the Lord your God gives you.

13 "You shall not murder.

14 "You shall not commit adultery.

15 "You shall not steal.

16 "You shall not bear false witness against your neighbor.

17 "You shall not covet your neighbor's house; you shall not covet your neighbor's wife or his male servant or his female

*servant or his ox or his donkey or anything
that belongs to your neighbor." (Ex 20: 2
NASB)*

The severity of the penalties attached to those laws

are seen in Exodus 32:1-28 when three thousand are

executed for their disobedience. Then again with the

punishments throughout Israel's history.

The Lord's Righteousness is in His Laws of

Creation, the Universe, Heaven, Earth and mankind.

David, Ezra and Jeremiah all declare the Lord's

Righteousness.

> *"Jehovah Sidkenu, the Lord our
> Righteousness" (Jeremiah 23:6, TLV)*

His Justice and thereby Righteousness is in His

enforcing His laws. Satan knew God had to enforce and

carry through on His righteousness by enforcing justice and

judgment. Satan counted on God's righteousness.

In Eden this caused mankind to become subjected to the death penalty. Satan tried to kill off God's favorite creation, and force God to do it! By subjecting mankind to the penalties of God's Law, the Lord's Righteous Justice demands any breach of God's law have the proper and just punishment imposed. Satan's trick would have worked if not for God's love of mankind.

> *"For God so loved the world, that He gave His only begotten Son, that whoever believes in Him shall not perish, but have eternal life. 17 For God did not send the Son into the world to judge the world, but that the world might be saved through Him. 18 He who believes in Him is not judged; he who does not believe has been judged already, because he has not believed in the name of the only begotten Son of God. (John 3:16 NASB)*

God took on Himself our death penalty; He suffered His Own Righteous Justice for our sake. Mankind was given the death penalty for the sin of Adam and Eve and all subsequent sins we all have accumulated in our lives.

Throughout the Bible we are reassured the evil will get their reward; they will finally pay for their ungodly thoughts, words and deeds. There are examples listed but the ultimate example of God's Righteousness and Justice is the fact He took on Himself the penalty ordained by His Own Law. The Law had to be upheld. God made the Law. God is Sovereign. A just and righteous sovereign cannot abrogate his or her own law as personal desire warrants. That action turns the realm into a realm of anarchy, a place where laws are random or subject to whims and uncontrolled emotion in power.

That is NOT God as we know from the Scriptures. God is Sovereign; the Lord is King of Kings. King means a monarchy; this is diametrically opposed to anarchy. A monarchy is difficult for today's Western culture to understand with our focus on democracy and representative governments, "republics". In the end, God's Law MUST be obeyed. So, God Himself loved and cared so much for His creation "man", He personally took our place and suffered our penalty of death. Why?

For one, God did this to show that NO one escapes the law; no one escapes the judgment mentioned earlier. Only by the forgiveness offered through accepting the blood of the sacrificed Messiah can the ultimate punishment be averted. Why God did this goes to His mercy.

While pondering this idea of righteousness, an interesting relationship showed up regarding righteousness and justice. The two concepts are completely interrelated and implicitly rely on each other.

Consider:

- ❖ Real Justice proves True Righteousness,

- ❖ True Righteousness demands Real Justice

- ❖ Justice requires Righteousness to be able to carry out true Justice

- ❖ Righteousness requires Justice to enforce true Righteousness.

- ❖ Without Justice there can be no Righteousness.

- ❖ In the same way, without Righteousness there can be no Justice.

- ❖ These two attributes of God's Nature are completely and inextricably intertwined.

- ❖ God's Holiness is demonstrative of His Righteousness; in this sense justice may be regarded as the actual execution of His Righteousness. God therefore is the

Supreme Judge, and the epitome of

Righteousness.

Revenge, retribution or logical conclusion?

The force of retribution is undeniable in Scripture as God is repeatedly taking ownership of vengeance or "retribution" *"Vengeance is Mine, I will repay saith the Lord"*. An extremely famous scientist and yet little known amazingly passionate Biblical scholar summed it up very well "for every action there is an equal and opposite reaction", Sir Isaac Newton. Many will call it "Karma", or "what goes around comes around". Regardless of how it is named, the force of retribution is understood everywhere.

It is this same "karma" which answers the next portion, the necessity of the Scriptures, thereby the knowledge of God and His commands, *the knowledge of good and evil*. Moral degeneracy acts like a cancer destroying silently from within. Like hatred or gluttonous lusts for food, power, sex, revenge, self-satisfaction, self-aggrandizement, self, this all separates us from God. Can there be any greater depth one can fall to than separation from God? He doesn't do that to us, we do it to ourselves. That's how it works, that's why Satan doesn't need to do anything but help us to do what we want for ourselves, as demonstrated in Eden. As individual humans we receive the effect of the cause we put in place in our lives; the effect of those things which we put in place of God in our lives, the "idols" of our vanities.

Depravity

Depravity, this is not only to mean that man is as bad as he can be; which is pretty low as anyone who has seen the internet can easily attest to. It is how is really the levels of depravity man can sink to; but in a Biblical sense it is more relevant to the depravity of man, as being man is as bad off as he can be. In other words, man is in as bad a situation as he could ever be in. Our sinful, depraved nature has separated us from God. What can be worse than separation from God? The life of man as it is, is in a situation where it gets worse every day as we walk ourselves further and further away from God. All the while, God is waiting for us to turn back to him.

This all stems from what happened in the Garden of Eden. Where God made man with His desire for man to walk together with Him. Instead, through Adam's sin, all of mankind has inherited this sinful nature. This has become life as it is; a creature beloved by God, who through Adam has turned away from that love.

The doctrine of depravity includes a variety of components. On one level we individually experience depravity and are individually sinful. On another it is collectively, we are all sinful due to our nature of sin which all of us inherited. This shows up as we collectively, in our nations are sinful. We enact man-made laws which "legislate" away God's commands and intentions.

Then on another level we are condemned through sin, condemned by God for what happened in Eden, again inheriting a sinful nature. And still on another level we are forever lost, stray sheep blindly wandering in sin; waiting for the strike at any moment of the devouring wolves or lions of Satan. This is life as it is for man and has been since his fall from the grace of God in the Garden.

This encompassing umbrella of sin covers all of us; we are all under the nature and concepts of sin. Sin can be seen in many forms, all of which are against God's Divine Will and purpose for man, life as it should be. These include such sinful acts as Adultery, fornication, uncleanness, lasciviousness, idolatry, witchcraft, hatred, variance, emulations, wrath, strife, sedition, heresies, envying, murders, drunkenness, reveling, dishonors to not only ourselves but to God as our Creator. Yeshua taught we do not have to actually commit these actions, but merely to think of them, to ponder them is just as bad as committing them in action. It is from our hearts these thoughts emulate and later turn into actions.

The wage of sin is death as we know. For this God has condemned man through sin to death. Sin has corrupted man as any cancerous disease. It eats at man bit by bit until the whole is worthless. This is the state of sin within which man exists.

This death is not only a physical death, which after Eden man is no longer an immortal, to eternally be with God. Man is now dead spiritually as well. Man not only dies when the heart stops, but there is no life in him. Our bodies are not the temples of God as our life should be, but are the white sepulchers or tombs, full of already dead bones, spiritless, Godless.

It is only through Messiah Yeshua that this condemnation is lifted. That the penalty inherited through Adam is removed and we can get a glimpse again of life as God intended, as it should be. Through the sacrifice on the execution stake, we are no longer under the power of Satan. No longer forced to see life as it is, living in the dominion of Satan under his constant control and influence. Only through the shed blood of the Messiah has life been transformed; to once again be able to walk with God in harmony. But this is not an immediate or simple transformation; it requires vigilance, daily thought and prayer and focus on God the Father through His Only Son Messiah Yeshua, our life as it should be. Satan is constantly trying to regain control over us, so we fight against principalities, powers, dominions.

We wander the world, lost sheep, food for ravenous wolves. Then we hear the voice of our Shepherd, calling to us to turn again towards Him, to turn away from our depravities and our selfish, self-motivated paths taking us away from Him. We turn from our lusts, desires of the heart which comes from our sinful nature, our inheritance. And thus, we undo that which was done in Eden by our primary ancestor Adam. We once again can have life as it should be, a member of the Divine Flock. That life can only come through belief and faith in the shed blood of our savior, our messiah Yeshua.

At one point all men believed in God, this is historically true, the study of any ancient culture demands the study of their religion as well; it's what made them think and act the way they did. It's what drove the ancient world and cultures. Belief in a God built the pyramids, the Taj Mahal, the Parthenon, Temple of Athena, Zeus and so on and more recently and most notably in Honor of the Lord, St Peter's in Rome, St John's in NY, St. Paul's and Westminster Abbey in England and even more importantly the Temple of Solomon and later the Herodian Temple.

As far back as any carved or painted rock, the belief in a higher being was there. Scriptures are the speaking points God has intended for us. They are the "rules" for survival in this world. When we warn our children not to put their hands in the fire, it is not intended to be mean but a warning to prevent their getting hurt. When people disbelieve (as so many do regarding God and Scriptures) they do it despite the warnings only to receive the natural consequences of the actions.

If we do something which is disobedient to God's commands, there is a natural consequence to the disobedience. It is not necessarily a punishment or God "being mean"; we were warned that there will be consequences to our disobedience our actions. Is there any surprise when a thief is caught and put in jail? There is a law and to that law there is a consequence for violating it. This is the same concept. With immorality there comes with it diseases, confusions, depressions, self-identity problems. There is also the disintegration of the family which then erodes the community as a whole. With uncleanness there is again a variety of diseases, illnesses and similar aftereffects. These are not "judgments of God" but a natural progression of cause and effect. This can include eating the wrong foods, as that can carry with it food poisoning and even death. On point to this are the Kosher rules which mainly deal with a clean and healthy food supply.

The rules were written long before refrigeration, antibiotics, sterilizers like bleach and other modern discoveries. The rules were God's warnings of not to put our hands into the flame as we could get "burned". Pork had the Trichinosis worm as well as dozens of other very serious diseases. Other animals had the potential for parasites, heart and intestinal worms and similar dangers. The Bible did not go into microbial details, it just said "don't eat these things". The term "you are what you eat" is perfectly applicable. On the unclean food list are all the bottom feeding animals. They are the world's cleanup crew eating the feces and other rotting debris. These are not to be eaten. You are what you eat.

All these are results from a common pattern of "cause and effect" and not necessarily of a higher judgment; though that still is possible depending on the situation, a situation only the higher power knows. Can we escape such a judgment? Yes, by faith, faith in the one who took the judgment upon Himself for our sinfulness.

Each of these demonstrates God is the final Judge. It is only through His righteousness, wisdom and knowledge can true justice and judgment take place. His judgment has the potential to be fierce, harsh and angry. It also can be merciful and caring. In Eden it was sudden, swift and both harsh and merciful. He could have immediately killed Adam and Eve, but that was not His desire as we know. He wanted to dwell with man. He also was not about to let that sly serpent get away with his attempts to thwart God's will. So, God Himself stepped into the mix personally and stepped on the head of the serpent.

This should show, we cannot escape God's final judgment except through the shed blood of His Son. We as imperfect humans have sinned and failed Him. We are incapable of any defense when we appear before His throne. We can say "I'm sorry" but it's too late for such a meager response at that point. What can one say when the Great Judge reminds us: "You were warned, but you did not heed the warning? You were told but you REFUSED to listen." And as we would be saying "I'm sorry" so would God also be saying how sorry He was; sorry we did not heed His continual warnings or take the chance provided by Him through His Son's sacrifice for us. Those poor souls would then sadly become eternally separated from Him. It is a judgment not by Him, but one we put upon ourselves through our actions.

The lifelong unrepentant sinners caused the judgment to come upon them by never accepting God's way out of eternal condemnation.

Going back to Adam and Eve, Scriptures are quite clear as well as human history that no one can escape God's righteous judgment. They, by their actions fell under that judgment. Their innocence was lost, they were now guilty beyond any doubt and thus were exposed to their fate.

This fate was one which required the ultimate penalty of death. But God had other plans. He wasn't going to fall into the scheme the Adversary had concocted and kill the very first of His new creation "Man" and thereby ending mankind's future existence. God took on the penalty Himself and thus paid the death penalty personally and completely. He took our place.

This is an interesting point which is readily visible in the Old Testament. It shows how the New Testament is in the Old though not always obvious. It takes a little research to find this out.

Chapter 4: The Trial

Intro - Putting it All Together

Now it is time to put all the pieces together and see if the case has been made.

Once again, let us introduce those involved.

Individual #1: Adam, the first man, from the Hebrew "ha Adam" for "the man" הָאָדָם.

Individual #2: The first woman, not yet named Eve Adam's help mate, הָאִשָּׁה the woman.

Individual #3: The Serpent, נָחָשׁ "nachash" to some "satan".

The first two individuals involved are obviously not present to answer any new questions, so their original testimonies and actions are the only evidence available. The third, the serpent is not about to answer honestly or truthfully.

Something happened and God, already knowing all the details and answers proceeded to have a trial.

The defendants are put on trial.

The trial begins as God questions the witnesses. Bear in mind, God already knows the answers to all questions, so the point of the question is always the subject of the question itself.

Adam takes the stand first.

> Then Adonai Elohim called to the man and He said to him, "Where are you?" 10 Then he said, "Your sound—I heard it in the garden and I was afraid. Because I am naked, I hid myself." 11 Then He said, "Who told you that you are naked? Have you eaten from the Tree from which I commanded you not to eat?" 12 Then the man said, "The woman whom You gave to be with me—she gave me of the Tree, and I ate." (Genesis 3:9 TLV)

Adam as the man was to give Eve strength as God gives us strength (energy), support and protection. Adam was to protect the family, including protecting Eve from the serpent's deception. What Adam did means he failed in the very least these areas.

Eve takes the stand.

> *Adonai Elohim said to the woman, "What did you do?" The woman said, "The serpent deceived me, and I ate." (Gen 3:13 TLV)*

(A fascinating point in all this is, how both of them blamed someone else. Adam blamed Eve and Eve blamed the serpent.)

What did Eve do that is sinful? She as the first woman was supposed to encapsulate the essence of woman, the quintessential mother of all human life. What could she have done that goes against the essence of her being a woman, that of nurturing, caring, raising children, of providing the perfect environment for growth of life, the future? She was to be Adam's partner in their existence together in the garden, dwelling together with God.

What was God's very first command? It was to go forth, be fruitful and multiply and to fill the Earth. A command He gave them personally and directly. What they did must have violated this very first and basic command.

God gave them very simple rules. Along with the command to be fruitful and multiply, their sustenance was to eat the fruit of all the trees except one. They were told in no uncertain terms not to eat of one particular tree, the one of the "knowledge of good and evil". As a typical human and the result of being told not to do something, they quickly set about making their way to it.

What did Adam and Eve do that was so horrific? The act being the absolute opposite of their being created in the first place. It must have been something which was the exact opposite of God's Natural Law and Will.

These are the two who perpetrated the so-called sin or "crime". There is one other character involved, the "serpent" who it is understood to be "Satan". The serpent beguiled Eve into disobedience; she then lured Adam to be her accomplice. What is still unknown is, accomplice to what?

Unlike modern "jurist-prudence", the Biblical trials were to be quick with punishment handed down soon after the judgment is made. As each one is interrogated, their particular punishment for disobedience is immediately handed down.

Crime and Punishment

God is a just God; therefore, the punishment must fit the crime. The results of the actions must therefore be the evidence of the action, just as a blood splattered body would reveal the scene of a murder; so too the punishment must reflect what the crime was.

> But if any harm follows, then you are to penalize life for life, 24 eye for an eye, tooth for a tooth, hand for hand, foot for foot, 25 burn for burn, wound for wound, blow for blow. (Ex 21:23 TLV)

A punishment must equal the crime. This is not to mean the retribution should be an exact match. It means it must not be more than the crime deserves. The penalty cannot be more severe than the crime itself. Their crime received the death penalty, so it was surely a capital crime.

By adding together, the results of the fall of man through the punitive and the corrective actions taken by

God, the original crime scene should be able to be reconstructed.

Instead of investigating by starting with a crime, finding out the suspects, making a case against them, having a trial, conviction and sentencing, this must be worked in the other direction. The punishment is known, the conviction was established, the case was made, those involved were identified. The question is, what did they do? What happened that started that chain of events?

The results of the incident are known. The disposition of the case, the resulting verdict and punishment for the illicit actions has been established. Motives are determined but what is not known is, what were the overt actions. What was the crime? What did they do?

There is a crime scene where every aspect of what took place is known except what actually took place. All the suspects are there in a line up, it is known who did it. The problem is, what did they do? They did something bad, but what did they do? This is the greatest conspiracy theory in history, the one which has been dogging mankind since, well since Original Sin.

Within the context of the related elements lies what Adam, and Eve did. Whatever that was, was against the Will of God. Eve sinned for considering the action, then proposing it to Adam, subsequently Adam failed in stopping Eve from this mysterious act by participating in it. Not only having failed to stop it, he went so far as to participate. What was it?

The only way to find the clues is from the many books and clues contained in the Bible. Not only the stories in the Bible, but the words used, how they are used and their interconnection. Whatever those two did upset all of God's creation and has caused the suffering we see and experience every day on all levels. What was it?

They did learn of death as a result.

Looking at the setting, Adam, (a man), Eve, (a woman), what does a man and a woman do best? They make more men and women. However, there were still no people other than Adam and Eve. Also, Adam did not "know" Eve until AFTER the fall, original sin, "the crime". Therefore, what they did must not include any of these elements.

Later, after being cast out from the garden, Adam works with Eve to start and raise a family. However, that family is fraught with destruction as a result of their fall from Grace. This again means their actions predate their family and its family structure. This is demonstrated in the book of Genesis.

The verdict was decided, and God's righteous judgment was immediately handed down. What were the punishments?

Sentence is handed down.

The Serpent:

Adonai Elohim said to the serpent, "Because you did this, cursed are you above all the livestock and above every animal of the field. On your belly will you go, and dust will you eat all the days of your life. 15 I will put animosity between you and the woman—between your seed and her seed. He will crush your head, and you will crush his heel. (Gen 3:14 TLV)

The Woman:

To the woman He said, "I will greatly increase your pain from conception to labor, in pain will you give birth to children. Your desire will be toward your husband, yet he must rule over you." (Gen 3:16 TLV)

Adam

Then to the man He said, "Because you listened to your wife's voice and ate of the tree which I commanded you, saying, 'You must not eat of it': Cursed is the ground because of you—with pain will you eat of it all the days of your life. 18 Thorns and thistles will sprout for you. You will eat the plants of the field, 19 By the sweat of your brow will you eat food, until you return to the ground, since from it were you taken. For you are dust, and to dust will you return." (Gen 3:17 TLV)

Then they were cast out of the garden and prevented from ever returning. What they did was obviously hateful to God and so He emptied the land of their presence.

God being a just and righteous God means these punishments or judgments must fit their specific actions.

The Punishments

First to the Serpent:

Adonai Elohim said to the serpent, "Because you did this, "Cursed are you above all the livestock and above every animal of the field. On your belly will you go, and dust will you eat all the days of your life. (Gen 3:14 TLV)

Mentioned previously is the role of the "serpent" or "dragon". Their enormous sizes are well known. However, for some reason, those large reptiles no longer exist. The ones which do today are low to the ground, virtually on their bellies. The legs of the Komodo Dragon, Crocodiles, Alligators, Iguanas and even serpents are short. They all "crawl on their bellies". Their curse of eating the dust of the ground points directly to their eating habits. What they ate must be a part of this scenario as food is the focal point of the temptation. This was explained earlier with the descriptions of serpents and dragons.

> *I will put animosity between you and the woman—between your seed and her seed. He will crush your head, and you will crush his heel. (Gen 14:15 TLV)*

There is now a natural fear between humans and reptiles. Some have overcome this, but by and large it is inherent to humans to fear these creatures. The reference is also the first reference to the coming of the Messiah to reverse all of this. "He will crush your head", Messiah will defeat all of the Adversary's evil leaders.

As one example, here is a foreshadow of the long line of evil leaders who come against God's people. This is a foreshadow of the coming leader who will come against God's people in the last days.

> The word of Adonai came to me saying: 2 "Son of man, set your face toward Gog of the land of Magog, <u>chief prince</u> of Meshech and Tubal (Ezekiel 38:1 TLV)

This passage is pretty much universally accepted to be referring to the leader of the armies who will come against Israel in the end times. The so called "Anti-Christ".

He bruised His heel.

The only physical evidence that exists today of Roman crucifixion is a single heel bone with a nail driven through it. The artifact was found in an ossuary or burial box and belonged to a criminal in Israel 2,000 years ago.

On the box was his name "Yehohanan" and is believed to have been in his mid-twenties. What his crime was is unknown, but the punishment is well known for the times. It was common practice for the Roman Empire to crucify someone. Thousands upon thousands were crucified by the Romans all across its empire.

With so many being crucified one would think there would be a great deal of evidence to this form of execution. That is not the case. There is one piece though, a heel bone with a nail through it. This is in Jerusalem. The original was buried as per Jewish custom, but before burial a 3D model was made and placed on view in the archaeology collections at Israel's national museum.

Normally the nails would have been removed at the time the body was taken off the cross or execution stake. In this case, the nail tip was bent sufficiently enough and apparently unable to be easily removed. It was left in place and as a result there is one piece of evidence of how a person was crucified.

This one and only piece shows the heel was where the nails were driven through the foot. This location has a large nerve running through it and would have been significantly more painful than any other location in the foot. The pain would have been increased as the person would try and push down to lift them self-up to breath. The method of crucifixion was not just meant to be public but slow and painful. Driving a nail through this part of the foot would make it very slow and exceptionally painful.

Next to the Woman

> *To the woman He said, "I will greatly increase your pain from conception to labor, in pain will you give birth to children. Your desire will be toward your husband, yet he must rule over you." (Gen 3:16 TLV)*

Here in lies the biggest clue as to what took place. From here on the evidence will continue mount exponentially to confirm the conclusion.

Eve's punishment was related to childbirth. Why? What could, or did she do that would imply childbirth? Her punishment was "increased pain" from conception to labor. Increased pain automatically implies such an event must have taken place already. A child must have already been conceived and given birth. Nothing in these particular chapters speak of a childbirth, just their punishments.

Added to the punishment of increased pain in birth is the desire for her husband, implying she would now want to become pregnant more readily and often. At the same time her husband Adam would now have dominion over her. She is now to be subservient to her husband.

What must be stressed here is this was never to imply the husband was to be a domineering tyrant. Quite the contrary. He was to be head of the family. His role was to be similar to God the Father who set forth the rules / laws or instructions for the family; the wife included. This is exemplified by the description of the husband and wife in a number of books.

> *Wives, be subject to your own husbands, as to the Lord. 23 For the husband is the head of the wife, as Christ also is the head of the church, He Himself being the Savior of the body. 24 But as the church is subject to Christ, so also the wives ought to be to their husbands in everything. 25 Husbands, love your wives, just as Christ also loved the church and gave Himself up for her, (Ephesians 5:22 NASB)*

> *In the same way, you wives, be submissive to your own husbands so that even if any of them are disobedient to the word, they may be won without a word by the behavior of their wives, 2 as they observe your chaste and respectful behavior. 3 Your adornment must not be merely external—braiding the hair, and wearing gold jewelry, or putting on dresses; 4 but*

let it be the hidden person of the heart, with the imperishable quality of a gentle and quiet spirit, which is precious in the sight of God. 5 For in this way in former times the holy women also, who hoped in God, used to adorn themselves, being submissive to their own husbands; 6 just as Sarah obeyed Abraham, calling him lord, and you have become her children if you do what is right without being frightened by any fear. 7 You husbands in the same way, live with your wives in an understanding way, as with someone weaker, since she is a woman; and show her honor as a fellow heir of the grace of life, so that your prayers will not be hindered. (1 Peter 3:1 NASB emphasis mine)

It is clear how the commands in Genesis are carried forth. The wife is to submit to the husband in love and respect for his role as the head of the family. Coupled with that is the husband is to care for, protect, love and respect the wife as Yeshua did, going so far as to sacrificed himself for the wife's wellbeing. This explanation was added due to the misuse and misrepresentation of the concept of submission by the wife and rulership of the husband. At no time was it to be of evil or malicious intent, but that of love and respect by both parties.

Finally, to Adam, the man

> *Then to the man He said, "Because you listened to your wife's voice and ate of the tree which I commanded you, saying, 'You must not eat of it': Cursed is the ground because of you—with pain will you eat of it all the days of your life. 18 Thorns and thistles will sprout for you. You will eat the plants of the field, 19 By the sweat of your brow will you eat food, until you return to the ground, since from it were you taken. For you are dust, and to dust will you return." (Gen 3:17 TLV)*

Adam would now have to work for the family's food. No longer was food readily available. Eve and Adam had forsaken the food God supplied and instead had chosen something else in its place. That food being the "Fruit of the Tree of the Knowledge of Good and Evil".

Then they were cast out of the garden and prevented from ever returning. Only later were God's people allowed to return to the lands they were cast out of. Interestingly it will be shown they were cast out for precisely the same reason.

This basic motif will be repeated throughout the Bible as will be demonstrated in the next and final section.

God's First Commands

*God blessed them; and God said to them,
"Be fruitful and multiply, and fill the
earth, and subdue it; and rule over the fish
of the sea and over the birds of the sky and
over every living thing that moves on the
earth." (Gen 1:28 NASB)*

וַיְבָרֶךְ אֹתָם, אֱלֹהִים, וַיֹּאמֶר לָהֶם אֱלֹהִים פְּרוּ וּרְבוּ
וּמִלְאוּ אֶת-הָאָרֶץ, וְכִבְשֻׁהָ; וּרְדוּ בִּדְגַת הַיָּם, וּבְעוֹף
הַשָּׁמַיִם, וּבְכָל-חַיָּה, הָרֹמֶשֶׂת עַל-הָאָרֶץ

When the statement is made that Adam and Eve

violated God's Commands or disobeyed God, it cannot be

referring to the Davidic Covenant, the Ten

Commandments, the Abrahamic covenant or the Noahide

rules or anything other than what transpired between God

and Adam and Eve. None of the later Commands or

Instructions can be retrofitted back to Adam and Eve in the

Garden. This limits what God commanded to a few simple

rules or commands.

These are:

- ➤ Be fruitful and multiply.

- ➤ Replenish the earth and subdue it.

- ➤ Have dominion over:

  - ○ The fish of the sea

  - ○ The fowl of the air

  - ○ every living thing that creepeth upon the earth.

They were clearly not to the point of needing to replenish the earth. Nor had they the time yet to have dominion over the fish, fowl, and every living thing. They were new to the earth and the only commands of God's they could have broken would be related to the first set, that of being fruitful and multiplying.

They are the first commands given, to be fruitful and multiply. These two terms complement each other and refer to the same thing. They refer exclusively to having children. What Adam and Eve did must then relate to disobeying this very first of all commands to man? So, when it is stated they disobeyed God, these are the only rules which could have been disobeyed. There were no others yet to which they could have disobeyed.

The use of the word fruitful makes the direct connection to the idea of what the word fruit means or represents. In this case the most obvious is the forbidden fruit. The fruit of the womb. There is only one answer to this, they killed the first born of creation, the first fruit of the womb. They killed the Son of God at birth.

This may have a sound of finality to it but that is due to a human perspective. God is eternal, therefore so is His Son. He who was, and is, and is to come. All that was murdered was the human body, ark or tabernacle in which the Spirit of God would have resided.

Satan was then punished in such a way as to exemplify this. Instead of just one having the Spirit of God; through faith and trust in Messiah and His sacrifice each of us can receive this Spirit. Now instead of one there are potentially billions accumulatively over time.

Again, it all points to one thing, the sin of Adam and Eve was the murder of their first child, a virgin birth.

The plans in action revisited.

To recap, here are the plans again only this time the addition of the essence of what took place.

God's plan in short:

God would create a place for Him and His new creature "man(kind)" to dwell together in harmony, in a personal relationship

> *"I will dwell among the sons of Israel and will be their God. Exodus 29:45 NASB*
>
> *"They shall know that I am the LORD their God who brought them out of the land of Egypt, <u>that I might dwell among them</u>; I am the LORD their God. (Exodus 29:46 NASB)*
>
> *Moreover,<u> I will make My dwelling among you</u>, and My soul will not reject you. (Leviticus 26:11 NASB emphasis mine)*
>
> *"You shall send away both male and female; you shall send them outside the camp so that they will not defile <u>their</u>*

camp where I dwell in their midst."
(Numbers 5:3 NASB)

'You shall not defile the land in which you live, in the midst of which I dwell; for I the LORD am dwelling in the midst of the sons of Israel.'" (Numbers 35:34 NASB emphasis mine)

"I will dwell among the sons of Israel and will not forsake My people Israel." (1 Kings 6:13 NASB)

Then I will give them a heart to know Me—for I am Adonai—and they will be My people, and I will be their God. (Jeremiah 24:7 NASB emphasis mine)

I will be their God and they will be My people. Jeremiah (31:32 NASB emphasis mine emphasis mine)

Then they will be My people and I will be their God. (Ezekiel 37:23 NASB emphasis mine)

"My dwelling place also will be with them; and I will be their God, and they will be My people. (Ezekiel 37:27 NASB)

He said to me, "Son of man, this is the place of My throne and the place of the soles of My feet, *where I will dwell among the sons of Israel forever* And the house of Israel will not again defile My holy name, neither they nor their kings, by their harlotry and by the corpses of their kings when they die, (Ezekiel 43:7 NASB emphasis mine)

"Now let them put away their harlotry and the corpses of their kings far from Me; *and I will dwell among them forever.* (Ezekiel 43:9 NASB emphasis mine)

"Sing for joy and be glad, O daughter of Zion; *for behold I am coming and I will dwell in your midst,*" declares the LORD. "Many nations will join themselves to the LORD in that day and will become My people *Then I will dwell in your midst,* and you will know that the LORD of hosts has sent Me to you. (Zechariah 2:10-11 NASB emphasis mine)

And the Word became flesh, *and dwelt among us,* and we saw His glory, glory as of the only begotten from the Father, full of grace and truth. (John 1:14 NASB emphasis mine)

just as God said, "*I will dwell in them and walk among them; and I will be their God, and they shall be My people.* (2 Cor 6:16 NASB emphasis mine)

And I will be their God, and they shall be My people. (Hebrews 8:10 NASB emphasis mine)

And I heard a loud voice from the throne, saying, "Behold, the tabernacle of God is among men, and He will dwell among them, and they shall be His people, and God Himself will be among them, (Revelation 21:3 NASB emphasis mine)

It is clear, time and time again God states categorically His desire is to dwell with man. God would enter the world as a man as the Son of God and dwell or tabernacle with man.

The Adversary

In contrast Satan had a plan of his own. Satan always wanted to raise himself up to the throne of God.

How you have fallen from heaven, O Brightstar, son of the dawn! How you are cut down to the earth, you who made the nations prostrate! 13 You said in your heart: "I will ascend to heaven, I will exalt my throne above the stars of God. I will sit upon the mount of meeting, in the uttermost parts of the north. 14 I will ascend above the high places of the clouds—I will make myself like Elyon." (Isaiah 14:12 TLV)

Satan's plan stands in stark contrast to God's plan.

Satan was jealous of God's new favorite creature, "man".

Satan also did not like the idea of God becoming one of these creatures who would then rule over him. His was a plan born out of pride and jealousy.

For to which of the angels did He ever say, "You are My Son, today I have begotten You"? And again, "I will be a Father to Him And He shall be a Son to Me"? 6 And when He again brings the firstborn into the world, He says, "And let all the angels of God worship Him." (Hebrews 1:5 NASB)

Satan was jealous and had far too much pride to let this happen. So he sets his own plan in motion, to destroy this new creature.

Satan's plan was a direct manipulation and corruption of God's new favorite creature "man". This plan if successful would cause man to become sinful and thereby lose God's protection and become subject to God's judgment. The Adversary's plan then continued to develop.

5. Since Satan could not destroy man himself, the plan would need to cause God to destroy them. This could only happen if they lost their protection and fell under God's judgment.

6. The plan must then cause Adam and Eve to commit a capital crime, and thereby require the death penalty. In so doing, Satan would cause man to destroy himself at the onset of his

existence, before the species favored by God can grow and multiply.

7. Satan would need to be very subtle and avoid a direct challenge to God. Whatever he did, he needed to play on their naiveté and innocence.

And so, Satan put his plan in motion. God knew what Satan was up to and had a plan of His own to restore all things.

> *Heaven must receive Him, until the time of the restoration of all the things that God spoke about long ago through the mouth of His holy prophets. (Act 3:21 TLV)*

These are all the primary details of the case. What will follow in Section 4 will be closing arguments and final points to this case.

Chapter 5 Closing Arguments

Shadows, Types and Repeated Patterns

As explained earlier, the Bible used a system of repeated patterns. These can be foreshadowing things to come or reflections of things which have happened in the past, or both. There are many of these foreshadows, patterns and types overlapped throughout the Bible. To many these run parallel to each other as they depicted people, places, and events, past, present, and future. It is within the context of this thesis that many, if not most all connect or lead back to the events in the first few chapters in Genesis. That instead of paralleling each other, seemingly unrelated, they have a direct connection to each other and to the events in the Garden in Genesis.

Since this is all based on the sin committed in the Garden, this section will begin with the sacrifice to be performed for the covering of sins.

The Sin Sacrifice and Offering

The temporary covering of sin as depicted in Genesis with the covering of animal skins is brought to the forefront in the sacrifices detailed in the book of Leviticus. There are a number of sacrifices to be offered for the commission of sin. There are sins committed without knowing one has committed them. There are sins which are known, sins of the priest, sins of the nation and so on. What is important in these is not so much who committed them or if they were known. The main point is the details of the atoning sacrifice. This is where sin itself is revisited time and time again. Sin itself began in Eden as we know. Later it progressed into all aspects of human life, like a virus, morphing into a different form as it infects humanity.

You were running well; who hindered you from obeying the truth? 8 This persuasion did not come from Him who calls you. 9 A little leaven leavens the whole lump of dough. (Gal 5:7 NASB)

Leaven starts out as a small amount but eventually causes the entire lump of dough to increase in size exponentially. Similar to how viruses work in the human body. It is interesting to note the similarities in the Biblical references to sin and disease.

Many have not read through the offerings or sacrifices so they are included here from the New American Standard Version.

The Sin Offering

Then the Lord spoke to Moses, saying, 2 "Speak to the sons of Israel, saying, 'If a person sins unintentionally in any of the things which the Lord has commanded not to be done, and commits any of them, 3 if the anointed priest sins so as to bring guilt on the people, then let him offer to the

Lord a bull without defect as a sin offering for the sin he has committed. 4 He shall bring the bull to the doorway of the tent of meeting before the Lord, and he shall lay his hand on the head of the bull and slay the bull before the Lord. 5 Then the anointed priest is to take some of the blood of the bull and bring it to the tent of meeting, 6 and the priest shall dip his finger in the blood and sprinkle some of the blood seven times before the Lord, in front of the veil of the sanctuary. 7 The priest shall also put some of the blood on the horns of the altar of fragrant incense which is before the Lord in the tent of meeting; and all the blood of the bull he shall pour out at the base of the altar of burnt offering which is at the doorway of the tent of meeting. 8 He shall remove from it all the fat of the bull of the sin offering: the fat that covers the entrails, and all the fat which is on the entrails, 9 and the two kidneys with the fat that is on them, which is on the loins, and the lobe of the liver, which he shall remove with the kidneys 10 (just as it is removed from the ox of the sacrifice of peace offerings), and the priest is to offer them up in smoke on the altar of burnt offering. 11 But the hide of the bull and all its flesh with its head and its legs and its entrails and its refuse, 12 that is, all the rest of the bull, he is to bring out to a clean place outside the camp where the ashes are poured out, and burn it on wood with fire; where the ashes are poured out it shall be burned.

13 'Now if the whole congregation of Israel commits error and the matter escapes the notice of the assembly, and they commit any of the things which the Lord has commanded not to be done, and they become guilty; 14 when the sin which they have committed becomes known, then the assembly shall offer a bull of the herd for a sin offering and bring it before the tent of meeting. 15 Then the elders of the congregation shall lay their hands on the head of the bull before the Lord, and the bull shall be slain before the Lord. 16 Then the anointed priest is to bring some of the blood of the bull to the tent of meeting; 17 and the priest shall dip his finger in the blood and sprinkle it seven times before the Lord, in front of the veil. 18 He shall put some of the blood on the horns of the altar which is before the Lord in the tent of meeting; and all the blood he shall pour out at the base of the altar of burnt offering which is at the doorway of the tent of meeting. 19 He shall remove all its fat from it and offer it up in smoke on the altar. 20 He shall also do with the bull just as he did with the bull of the sin offering; thus, he shall do with it. So the priest shall make atonement for them, and they will be forgiven. 21 Then he is to bring out the bull to a place outside the camp and burn it as he burned the first bull; it is the sin offering for the assembly.

22 'When a leader sins and unintentionally does any one of all the things which the Lord his God has commanded not to be done, and he becomes guilty, 23 if his sin which he has committed is made known to him, he shall bring for his offering a goat, a male without defect. 24 He shall lay his hand on the head of the male goat and slay it in the place where they slay the burnt offering before the Lord; it is a sin offering. 25 Then the priest is to take some of the blood of the sin offering with his finger and put it on the horns of the altar of burnt offering; and the rest of its blood he shall pour out at the base of the altar of burnt offering. 26 All its fat he shall offer up in smoke on the altar as in the case of the fat of the sacrifice of peace offerings. Thus the priest shall make atonement for him in regard to his sin, and he will be forgiven.

27 'Now if anyone of the common people sins unintentionally in doing any of the things which the Lord has commanded not to be done, and becomes guilty, 28 if his sin which he has committed is made known to him, then he shall bring for his offering a goat, a female without defect, for his sin which he has committed. 29 He shall lay his hand on the head of the sin offering and slay the sin offering at the place of the burnt offering. 30 The priest shall take some of its blood with his finger and put it on the horns of the altar of burnt offering; and all the rest of its blood he shall pour out at the base of the altar. 31 Then he shall remove all its fat, just as the fat was removed from the sacrifice of peace offerings; and the priest shall offer it up in smoke on the altar for a soothing aroma to the Lord. Thus the priest shall make atonement for him, and he will be forgiven.

32 'But if he brings a lamb as his offering for a sin offering, he shall bring it, a female without defect. 33 He shall lay his hand on the head of the sin offering and slay it for a sin offering in the place where they slay the burnt offering. 34 The priest is to take some of the blood of the sin offering with his finger and put it on the horns of the altar of burnt offering, and all the rest of its blood he shall pour out at the base of the altar. 35 Then he shall remove all its fat, just as the fat of the lamb is removed from the sacrifice of the peace offerings, and the priest shall offer them up in smoke on the altar, on the offerings by fire to the Lord. Thus the priest shall make atonement for him in regard to his sin which he has committed, and he will be forgiven. (Leviticus 4:1-5:13 NASB)*

The Trespass Offering

'Now if a person sins after he hears a public adjuration to testify when he is a witness, whether he has seen or otherwise known, if he does not tell it, then he will bear his guilt. 2 Or if a person touches any unclean thing, whether a carcass of an unclean beast or the carcass of unclean *cattle or a carcass of unclean swarming things, though it is hidden from him and he is unclean, then he will be guilty. 3 Or if he touches human uncleanness, of whatever sort his uncleanness may be with which he becomes unclean, and it is hidden from him, and then he comes to know it, he will be guilty. 4 Or if a person swears thoughtlessly with his lips to do evil or to do good, in whatever matter a man may speak thoughtlessly with an oath, and it is hidden from him, and then he comes to know it, he will be guilty in one of these. 5 So it shall be when he becomes guilty in one of these, that he shall confess that in which he has sinned. 6 He shall also bring his guilt offering to the Lord for his sin which he has committed, a female from the flock, a lamb or a goat as a sin offering. So the priest shall make atonement on his behalf for his sin.*

7 'But if he cannot afford a lamb, then he shall bring to the Lord his guilt offering for that in which he has sinned, two turtledoves or two young pigeons, one for a sin offering and the other for a burnt offering. 8 He shall bring them to the priest, who shall offer first that which is for the sin offering and shall nip its head at the front of its neck, but he shall not sever it. 9 He shall also sprinkle some of the blood of the sin offering on the side of the altar, while the rest of the blood shall be drained out at the base of the altar: it is a sin offering. 10 The second he shall then prepare as a burnt offering according to the ordinance. So the priest shall make atonement on his behalf for his sin which he has committed, and it will be forgiven him.

11 'But if his means are insufficient for two turtledoves or two young pigeons, then for his offering for that which he has sinned, he shall bring the tenth of an ephah of fine flour for a sin offering; he shall not put oil on it or place incense on it, for it is a sin offering. 12 He shall bring it to the priest, and the priest shall take his handful of it as its memorial portion and offer it up in smoke on the altar, with the offerings of the Lord by fire: it is a sin offering. 13 So the priest shall make atonement for him concerning his sin which he has committed from one of these, and it will be forgiven him; then the rest

shall become the priest's, like the grain offering.'" (Lev 4:1-13 NASB)

The Law of the Sin Offering

The Law of the Sin Offering

Then the Lord spoke to Moses, saying, 25 "Speak to Aaron and to his sons, saying, 'This is the law of the sin offering: in the place where the burnt offering is slain the sin offering shall be slain before the Lord; it is most holy. 26 The priest who offers it for sin shall eat it. It shall be eaten in a holy place, in the court of the tent of meeting. 27 Anyone who touches its flesh will become consecrated; and when any of its blood splashes on a garment, in a holy place you shall wash what was splashed on. 28 Also the earthenware vessel in which it was boiled shall be broken; and if it was boiled in a bronze vessel, then it shall be scoured and rinsed in water. 29 Every male among the priests may eat of it; it is most holy. 30 But no sin offering of which any of the blood is brought into the tent of meeting to make atonement in the

holy place shall be eaten; it shall be
burned with fire. (Lev 6:24 NASB)

The New Testament makes an interesting statement
which confirms the connection to Eden.

But in those sacrifices there is a reminder
of sins year by year. (Hebrews 10:3
NASB)

A reminder of sins every year; sins continued every
year ever since Eden. The sacrifices are the reminder of the
continuation of human weakness and sinfulness. This
continuation of human weakness and sin has its starting
point in Eden with Adam and Eve. There is no argument to
where sin began.

At the presentation of the sacrifice the person
presenting the animal would lay their hands on the sacrifice
and symbolically pass their sins onto the sacrifice. The
most important aspect of all this is not so much the
different sins but the consistent elements of death, food and

blood. There was a lot of blood poured out at the slaying of one of these animals.   The lamb alone has about 5 liters of blood.

The role of the priest was to direct the sacrifice, not be the one to do it for the individual sinner. The individual who brought the sacrifice was to be the one who slew the animal, thereby being covered in the gushing blood. This was reflective of the nature of not only their sin but sin itself. This goes directly back to Eden where sin began.

The sacrifice was slaughtered, disemboweled and the pieces thrown in the fire as directed. Then the individual would go over to the bronze laver which was polished to the point of being a bronze mirror and would then proceed to wash the blood off. As they did this they looked into the water and would see themselves covered in the sign of sin. They were covered in blood. Again, this points directly to what, where and how sin began in Eden.

The depiction of being covered in blood as representative of sin can be seen in the first chapter of Isaiah.

לְכוּ-נָא וְנִוָּכְחָה, יֹאמַר יְהוָה; אִם-יִהְיוּ
חֲטָאֵיכֶם כַּשָּׁנִים כַּשֶּׁלֶג יַלְבִּינוּ, אִם-יַאְדִּימוּ כַתּוֹלָע
כַּצֶּמֶר יִהְיוּ

"Come now, let us reason together," says
Adonai. "Though your sins be like scarlet,
they will be as white as snow. Though they
be red like crimson, they will become like
wool.(Isaiah 1:18 TLV)

Contained in this word אִם-יַאְדִּ֨ימוּ is a variant of the word for blood.

Why is sin of any kind depicted as being blood red or covered in blood? The suggested reason is sin which began in Eden was a sin which covered Adam and Eve in blood and subsequently all of mankind. Thereby sin is depicted as being blood red. God tells us He will one day erase all sins, removing all the blood stain from our hands and lives, making them "white as wool". Just like the wool of a lamb so to speak.

Forbidden Fruit Decoded

What was that fruit? What was that tree? Where does the knowledge of good and evil come from? Basically, it comes from two places:

1) One is our conscience, our conscience tends to be our guide, kind of pushing and nudging in the right direction of good and away from evil. Where does our conscience emanate from? The Bible tells us it comes from the Holy Spirit.

2) The inspired Word of God, the Scriptures which come through men who have been inspired by the Holy Spirit. It is in the Scriptures that the aspects of good and evil are explained. This is the knowledge of good and evil and it comes from the Holy Spirit.

God passes the knowledge to us through the Holy Spirit.

So, what was or is the tree of the knowledge of good and evil and what is its fruit? The answers above show Holy Spirit is the Tree of the Knowledge of Good and Evil. The fruit of that tree, as the Bible teaches, is the Messiah, the Son of God. "The Holy Spirit will come upon you and you shall conceive a son…"

Again, using the Remez aspect of interpretation, a conclusion can be drawn that Yeshua, being the Messiah was this First Fruit. The First Born of Creation.

However, here is where the crime happens. He (Yeshua) is not only the first born but the first to die. *"As through one-man (Adam) death entered the world"*. Whose death? Who did Adam kill that death is attributed to him?

Some will rightly postulate it's our death, the loss of immortality, of death itself. However, what crime caused our death penalty? It must have been a capital crime of some sort. The crime is the murder of the First Fruit and it is that death which is where "death" enters the world. It is then repeated in the offspring of Adam and Eve when Cain slays Able.

Messiah is that First Fruit (of the womb), the First Born of Creation.

As one can quickly surmise from other comments, there is an obvious connection to the term fruits and first fruits and the related festival. It is a Biblical fact the Messiah is to be the "First Fruits of the Resurrection." Is this merely a coincidence that He is called the "First Fruit" as well as the First Born of Creation? Is it a coincidence that like a piece of fruit He is hung on a tree? Could this term be reflective of the first fruit mentioned in the Garden

of Eden, the "fruit of the tree of the knowledge of good and

evil"? The FIRST fruit of that tree?

> *For we know that the whole creation*
> *groans and suffers the pains of childbirth*
> *together until now. 23 And not only this,*
> *but also we ourselves, having the first*
> *fruits of the Spirit... (Romans 8:23 – 22*
> *NASB)*

Then by receiving Messiah into our hearts, we too

become a part of that "First Fruits."

> *By His will, He brought us forth by the*
> *word of truth, so that we might be a kind*
> *of first fruits of all He created. (James*
> *1:18 TLV).*

> *By His will, He brought us forth by the*
> *word of truth, so that we might be a kind*
> *of first fruits of all He created. (Romans*
> *11:16TLV)*

The food mentioned in Genesis, which is forbidden

to be eaten is specifically called: "The Fruit of the Tree of the Knowledge of Good and Evil." That is an interesting name for a food. It becomes even more interesting when one examines what the name actually means.

Again, this points to this tree as that of the Holy Spirit. Messiah said, He will send us a another who will be by our side and guide us; the "parakletos". This entity we know to be the Ruach Ha Kodesh or Holy Spirit, the "Spirit of God". As our guide the (Holy) Spirit will bring to mind those things we need to say. It will remind us of God's Instructions, how to live, act and be responsible disciples of the Lord. That is the "job" of the Holy Spirit. Our conscience, the source of our knowledge of good and evil.

> These things I have spoken to you while dwelling with you. 26 But the Helper, the Holy Spirit (Ruach ha-Kodesh) whom the Father will send in My name, will teach you everything and remind you of everything that I said to you. (John 14:25 TLV)

But when the Spirit of truth comes, He will guide you into all the truth. (John 16:13 TLV)

The Holy Spirit is the Tree of the Knowledge of

Good and Evil. The fruit of that tree, as the Bible teaches,

is the Messiah, Yeshua.

Mary said to the angel, "How can this be, since I am a virgin?" 35 The angel answered and said to her, "The Holy Spirit will come upon you, and the power of the Most High will overshadow you; and for that reason the holy Child shall be called the Son of God. (Luke 1:34 NASB)

The Holy Spirit IS the de facto other "parent" of

Messiah Yeshua.

In the Gospel Elizabeth praises Miriam who is

pregnant with the Messiah.

When Elizabeth heard Mary's greeting, the baby leaped in her womb; and Elizabeth was filled with the Holy Spirit. 42 And she cried out with a loud voice and said, "Blessed are you among women, and blessed is the fruit of your womb! (Luke 1:41 NASB)

The metaphor blatantly compares unborn Yeshua to a fruit. It is not a long stretch to say the "fruit" being referred to in Genesis is a child, a human child. The Child of God, the First Fruit, the First Born of Creation. The next verse now takes on a new layer of understanding.

> *"Sanctify to Me every firstborn, the first offspring of every womb among the sons of Israel, both of man and beast; it belongs to Me." (Exodus 13:2 NASB emphasis mine)*

Yeshua, the Son of God is the First Born of Creation, He is also the First Born of Miriam, and in relation to this thesis, the First Born of Eve.

Bear in mind God's original intention was to dwell here with man. This is demonstrated with Abraham who was "God's Friend". Then again when He dwelt with the Israelites in the wilderness.

God, as in the Garden of Eden spoke (which is the Word of God) with man, (Adam). The Word of God was in the Garden; therefore, Messiah was there with Adam and Eve but only as a voice. His intention was to be face to face with man, not just a voice.

But there was someone else there who was destined to try and circumvent God's plan. God was coming upon Eve as He did with Miriam, to dwell with man in and on God's creation. But Satan sought to stop this and so he tempted Eve to do it for him. This is Mankind's original sin.

If you have not put all the pieces together by now, here is what happened plainly spoken. Original Sin was an aborted birth, the slaying of an unborn / newborn child. In this case a Holy Child, the Son of God. Very similar to the concept in the story "Agnes of God" though that was supposedly by the angel Michael and really has no bearing on this thesis. In the case against Adam, Eve and the Serpent, the child was aborted at or just after the moment of birth, before being able to speak.

> *Like a lamb led to the slaughter, like a sheep before its shearers is silent, so He did not open His mouth (Isaiah 53:7 NASB)*

The birth of Immanuel (God with us) by Eve was aborted for food and to become "god like". The same temptations which were put to Yeshua in the wilderness.

The Serpent deceived Eve to think eating the young was a natural and good thing to do. The visual point of view at what is known as the crowning, (the beginning of the skull emerging at birth), would have appeared very similar to that of an egg coming out. Only it was the head of a baby. In modern terms this would be considered a "partial birth" abortion. (A process where the baby's head comes out of the mother, the spinal column is severed, a

hole is pierced into the back of the skull and the brain

material sucked out with a vacuum.)

It was common for the giant "serpents" or reptiles,

to eat their young. Eve didn't know what she was doing.

As Hosea puts it:

> *My people are destroyed for lack of knowledge; because you have rejected knowledge, (Hosea 4:6 TLV)*

Eve was having a baby.

> *Before she was in labor, she gave birth. Before her pain came, she delivered a male child. (Isaiah 66:7 TLV)*

She didn't know what it was or what to do with it.

She had a choice to kiss or murder and eat it. Then like the

larger reptiles (especially of the period), who eat the eggs

of their young as well as their young she and Adam killed

the child for food. It wasn't their own idea, but was

suggested through the beguiling of the Serpent, a.k.a. "Satan".

It is well known in the world of Paleontology of how prehistoric "dinosaurs" ate their young. In a paper by a leading Paleontologist, the fact of the larger dinosaurs eating the young was or is evidenced by the lack of the remains of any young or juvenile dinosaurs. This is common among predatory animals today as well. The young and weak are attacked for food as they are the most vulnerable and least able to defend themselves.

Notice the comment from the book of Isaiah about the time of restoration when Messiah has finally come to restore Creation to its original state.

> *The wolf will dwell with the lamb, the leopard will lie down with the kid, the calf and the young lion and the yearling together, and a little child will lead them. 7 The cow and the bear will graze, their*

young ones lie down together, and the lion will eat straw like an ox. 8 A nursing child will play by a cobra's hole, and a weaned child will put his hand into a viper's den. 9 They will not hurt or destroy in all My holy mountain, for the earth will be full of the knowledge of Adonai, as the waters cover the sea. (Isaiah 11:6 TLV)

The passage points to a time when no longer will humans and animals be against each other. That is a truly inspiring idea but, more importantly is the relationship between the animals themselves. No longer will the young be fed upon. It's not pointing to animals necessarily feeding on each other and thereby instilling fear from predators in general. Instead, it's pointing to the assault and feeding on the young. It's a reflection of Original Sin. In each of the cases listed it points to the young as having been victimized.

When will this occur? After the First Born of Creation has returned to restore all things. Before the fall, animals apparently did not prey on the young of any species. After the fall of man, they did this and still do to this day.

Satan knew how this worked; he knew the creature "man" would be completely vulnerable at birth and how the parents would normally and inherently protect it. This is why the disguise of a serpent was used by Satan to tempt Eve to kill and eat her first born. The First Born of the Holy Spirit; the First Born of Creation. After having seen reptiles (serpents), eat the eggs out of their own nests the idea was planted.

The First Born

The Messiah is the first born of all creation.

For all the firstborn are Mine; on the day that I struck down all the firstborn in the land of Egypt, I sanctified to Myself all the firstborn in Israel, from man to beast. They shall be Mine; I am the Lord."
(Numbers 3:13 NASB)

He is the image of the invisible God, the firstborn of all creation. (Col 1:15 NASB)

However, if we look at the story of Creation, the first born is Cain. Where is Yeshua? Cain is not a Biblical type for Yeshua and Yeshua certainly wasn't reflective of Cain. Adam and Eve were "Created" not born. So that leaves them out. There's no one else present but God, Elohim.

Where or how then is Yeshua as the first born? Some say it shows His preeminence. Still others argue Paul

was making what could be termed a "Biblical Conflict".
That he was presenting Yeshua as both the creator and the
created. This is not a "conflict" but a statement of what
took place. Yeshua is Creator and was also "born of"
Miriam, part of the Creation. So, the argument He could
not be the "First Born of Creation" in its literal sense is a
false argument. This means He could have been the first
born of Creation. He can be the Creator and still be part of
the creation.

> *"Before she travailed, she brought forth;*
> *Before her pain came, she gave birth to a*
> *boy. 8 "Who has heard such a thing? Who*
> *has seen such things? (Isaiah 66:7 NASB)*

Who has heard such a thing, seen such things? No
one. That statement in Isaiah implies only one conclusion.
There is only one terrifying, horrific answer, they murdered
their first born. Cain is the second conception of Eve only

now it is by Adam. The genetic sin is passed on to Cain. That first inherited sin is murder.

The First Born was to be conceived by God as it was with Miriam in Bethlehem.

Cain ends up with the same blood on his hands as well for murdering his own brother. The children learn from their parents. "Teach them in their youth" the Bible says. Through Adam death entered the world and Cain carried on that legacy.

Eve and Adam didn't nurture and protect the child but killed it instead. It was an order they both were to follow, be fruitful and multiply. That was one of the few rules God laid down for them at the very beginning. Their actions violated these Commands as well as circumvented God's motive or plan for His love of man.

Satan tempted Eve, who in turn tempted Adam. Satan's motive and plan are apparent and is why Eve was tempted the way she was. After which the First born of

Creation was murdered at the moment of birth.

The death is the sin passed down from Adam and

Eve. The first born of creation was the first to die, the first

aborted.

> *And all the people said, "His blood shall*
> *be on us and on our children!" (Matthew*
> *27: 25 NASB)*

This is the curse handed down from Eden and is

repeated with Yeshua's execution.

Remember the words of Yeshua on the cross:

> *Two others also, who were criminals,*
> *were being led away to be put to death*
> *with Him. 33 When they came to the place*
> *called the Skull, there they crucified Him*
> *and the criminals, one on the right and the*
> *other on the left. 34 But Jesus was saying,*
> *"Father, forgive them; for they do not*
> *know what they are doing." (Luke 23:32*
> *NASB)*

What is fascinating is how He dies between two criminals or sinners so to speak. In Eden this is precisely what would have been happening. At that moment they would have been considered criminals and sinners. The child would have died between them. Again, this is all a replay of Eden for the purpose of undoing what took place there.

Then at the end he states, "it is accomplished". What was accomplished? What was it that was finished? The atonement for sin was accomplished. The sin of Adam and Eve and their actions in Eden was resolved. The penalty was paid. It was accomplished, and the case closed, it is finished.

The original reason for Messiah to come into this world the way He did was to atone for the sinful action which took place in Eden. On the Cross or Execution Stake He was asking for the forgiveness of that sin. His execution was the blood atonement required by God's judgment.

The atonement for the murder of the First Born of Creation. The sin Adam and Eve committed in the Garden of Eden. What was that action? The abortion of the First-Born child by the first created parents.

Immanuel was dead! Satan had tricked man into killing God's perpetual human incarnation at the moment of birth.

> *and they will mourn for Him, as one mourns for an only son, and they will weep bitterly over Him like the bitter weeping over a firstborn. (Zechariah 12:10 NASB)*

They didn't initially weep like a parent <u>weeps for an only child</u>. Instead, they dodged the questions asked at their trial. And yet at that point, it was their only child. The only child born to creation, the First Born of Creation.

The entire Bible points to the death of Messiah, both forwards and backwards!

The covering with skin not only demonstrates the need for blood atonement, a payment in blood for bloodshed, but it is also a blatant rebuke of their actions. God was ostensibly saying by this action: You want to act like beasts, then dress and look like one! You will wear hair to cover what you call your nakedness like all the other beasts of the Earth. It also becomes a foreshadow of the sacrificial system where they become covered in animal's blood and animals are killed for said covering.

This anger and judgment by God are the same anger God had when He made the Children of Israel in the desert not only grind the golden calf up but made them drink the powdered gold in their water. They were made to actually eat their sin. This too is a reflection of the sin of Adam and Eve. Their sin was what they ate. Shadowing Adam and

Eve, the Israelites ate an image of a young bull. The calf reflecting a child and gold reflecting divinity. This was another example of how the two first people ate their young, one of divine origin.

A woman's increased sorrow is shown every time a woman sees a suffering child or even a "puppy" or similar young creature, her sorrow over shadowing the man's. It is a reminder of what was done: "The Original Sin," she killed her first (un)born child.

Here are a few more passages which reflect on the role of the first born and God's ownership of them. These precisely parallel the First Born of Creation in Eden.

> As it is written in the Torah of Adonai, "Every firstborn male that opens the womb shall be called holy to Adonai." (Luke 2:23 TLV)

> "Consecrate to Me all the firstborn, from every womb of Bnei-Yisrael, both men and

animals—this is Mine." (Exodus 13:2 TLV)

you are to set apart to Adonai every firstborn from the womb, and every firstborn male animal you have will be Adonai's. 13 Every firstborn donkey you are to redeem with a lamb, and if you do not redeem it, then you are to break its neck. But you are to redeem every firstborn male among your sons. (Exodus 13: 12 TLV emphasis mine)

and when Pharaoh refused to let us go, Adonai slew all the firstborn in the land of Egypt, both men and animals. So, I sacrifice to Adonai all firstborn males, but I redeem the firstborn of my sons.' (Exodus 13:15 TLV)

Notice how the animals are to be sacrificed but the children specifically are not. They are to be "redeemed". Throughout the Bible God abhors the killing of the children, especially the first born. It is a repeated theme.

Biblical Women

The women are in the forefront of this as they are the ones entrusted with giving birth. The bringing forth of new life, raising and protecting it. How each came to be significant persons of the Bible shows the strength and character of each one. If we look at different women or more specifically the mothers spoken of in the Bible, a pattern can be seen running in the background.

Starting with the birth of Isaac we see how his birth was completely unplanned by the parents. Sarah even went so far as to laugh at the mere thought of having a baby at her age of 90. The Angel of the Lord having heard her laugh, rebuked her and told her He would return at the "appointed time" for the child's birth.

Later Isaac's son Jacob marries Leah and Rachel. Rachel is initially barren; she did not have children. However, after praying for such an event she gives birth to Joseph and later Benjamin. Joseph being the primary example or type for the Suffering Servant of the coming Messiah.

Moving on to the child Moses, the girl who pulled him from the river would have been young and unmarried at that time. With probably no immediate plans of being a parent and yet she takes on that role. Then suddenly she adopts a newborn baby to raise as her own. However, her being so young and not having given birth as yet was unable to nurse the child. Instead the baby Moses was actually nursed and cared for by his birth mother using his older sister Miriam as an emissary to the Egyptian princess.

Elizabeth, the mother of John the Baptist was also in her older years when she gave birth to her first-born son. It was such a surprise his father Zacharias didn't believe it and was made mute until the time the child was named by his mother Elizabeth.

Most importantly is Miriam, the mother of Yeshua. She was suddenly visited by an angel and told she was going to have a baby who would then be known as the Son of God, Immanuel (God with us) and to name Him Yeshua (God's salvation). Her pregnancy is truly the most surprising as she was still as yet an unmarried virgin.

True it is normally a surprise for the woman to find out she is pregnant. In these cases, though, the situations are far from the normal surprise. Sarah was by far too old. Rachel was older and had until that point been barren. The woman who raised Moses was a teenager who suddenly found and decided to raise the baby; drawing him from the waters. Elizabeth was also beyond child bearing years and like Sarah had not had any children previously. Lastly Miriam was still an unmarried virgin. God creates life where there is no life.

Eve is one of these very special women in the Bible. Eve and Miriam are the two main women and appear to parallel and yet contrast each other. They are both supposed to represent the epitome of a woman. However, there is a drastic difference. Eve being the mother of all living sinned greatly. Her actions condemning all of mankind and creation to certain death.

Whereas Miriam was different and as a result she is venerated as being pure and without sin. She not only brought forth life but brought forth the savior and restorer of all life; especially eternal life for all who believe.

Miriam submitted herself to God's Will as opposed to Eve who defied and disobeyed it. Miriam had complete faith and trust in God's Word. Eve did not.

What sin could Eve have done that Miriam did not? The difference is rather obvious. If Miriam's submission to God's Will resulted in her giving birth to the child of God, then the only polar opposite would be Eve murdered the child.

This is the central point of this thesis. Miriam gave life, Eve gave death.

Solomon's Decision

King Solomon was supposed to be the wisest of all the people throughout history. As king of Israel he must have made thousands of decisions. But in the Bible only one is recorded in detail. One of all he had made stands out in particular and is detailed in the book of 1-Kings. The way it is presented it seems as though it is his first "great" or "wise" decision, I'm sure he must have made many other decisions in his life, long before this particular one and many more afterwards. This one decision, however, is really not quite as "wise" as it may seem, though it is very clever. Its cleverness is wrapped up in a "trick" question.

The question is why? Why was this one decision of all the others made so unique? What is so significant about this interaction and decision that it stands out as such a wise decision? The Scriptures do not say it was his wisest decision, only that the people saw his wisdom through it.

Some of the story is rather, sorry to say "absurd" on its face. By this I mean, consider the second woman or prostitute. Ok, she's upset, she rolled over and killed her child allegedly by accident, that's understandable. But later, when confronted by the court of Solomon who offers to cut the living child in two, she agrees to it.

Is there really any sane woman who would say to cut a child in two so she could have or keep half of the child's "corpse"? She already has one dead child's body, so why want half of another? Especially when you consider the actual physical dynamics of half of a human body, child or otherwise. Compound this with the Torah and the commands against being around any dead body.

When thought through, it really doesn't make rational sense. It suggests the second woman wasn't just a prostitute but somewhat of a sociopath. It just seems bizarre any woman in her right mind would ask for half of a child's body. This all suggests a deeper meaning to the entire story itself.

The point of the story, besides showing off Solomon's wisdom and cleverness, is the determination of the rightful mother of the child.

First, what is Solomon's decision? This is what the Bible says happened.

What was that decision?

> *Later two prostitutes came to the king and stood before him. 17 One woman said: "My lord, please! This woman and I live in the same house, and I delivered a child while she was in the house. 18 On the third day after I gave birth, this woman also*

gave birth to a child. While we were together with no one else with us in the house, just the two of us in the house, 19 this woman's child died during the night, because she lay on top of him. 20 Then she got up in the middle of the night and took my son from my side while your handmaid was asleep. She laid him at her breast and laid her dead child at my breast. 21 When I rose in the morning to nurse my child, he had just died! But when I looked at him closely in the morning, I realized that he was not the son I had borne!" 22 But the other woman said, "No! For the living one is my son, and the dead one is your son!" But the first woman said, "No! The dead one is your son and the living one is my son!" Thus, they spoke before the king. 23 Then said the king: "The one says, 'This is my son who is living, and your son is the dead,' while the other says, 'No, but your son is the dead one and my son is the living one.'" 24 Then the king said: "Bring me a sword." So, they brought a sword before the king. 25 Then the king said: "Divide the living child in two, and give half to the one and half to the other." 26 Then the woman whose son was the living one spoke up to the king—for her heart grew tender for her son—and said, "My lord, please! Give her the living child! Only don't kill him!" But the other said, "It will be neither mine nor yours! Cut it in two!" 27 Then the king responded by saying, "Give her the living child and certainly don't kill him. She is the mother." 28 When all Israel heard of the verdict that the king had given, they were in awe of the king. For they saw that the wisdom of God was in him to administer justice. (1Kings 3:16 TLV)

Solomon's decision is still hailed today as an amazing and wise conclusion to handling the matter. Some may wish to debate this, but such a debate is purely academic and subjective.

The conflict is settled when King Solomon calls for a sword to sever the child in two and thus divide it between the two women. The mother of the dead child (the one who stole the living child), said yes killing the child, cutting it into two, thereby making sure neither would have it.

The other woman wailed and declared "NO!" as she did not want the child to die. It was her wish to just give the baby over to the other mother, thus allowing the child to live. Solomon heard this and made his decision and gave the first woman her living child, declaring this was truly the mother of the child; as she wanted the child to live and not die.

The Divine inspiration which inspired the story about this decision to be included must have had an intention of passing the wisdom contained therein to future generations. One possibility is this reflected Original Sin and the difference between a woman who is good and one who is evil. The fact both were prostitutes shows it had nothing to do with their habits or lifestyles. What was important was how they treated their child. Was the motive to preserve life or destroy it?

Solomon's decision shows who was the true mother, the one who preserved life. There is much more to this story, but this is the part which is on point to this discussion.

Women and Childbirth

The levels of depression a woman can have is also well known, especially after childbirth, this is as we know "postpartum depression" and has arguably led to infanticide on numerous occasions.

After having an abortion, woman have stated how they felt total emptiness unlike anything before. In some cases, as if their very soul had been taken; an inexplicable emptiness and so on. In one word "desolate".

Again, the correlation of "crime and punishment", "cause and effect" points backwards to the deed, Adam and Eve killed their first-born child. That child was to be as Isaiah said, "he shall be called Immanuel" meaning "God with us".

> Therefore Adonai Himself will give you a sign: Behold, the virgin (Heb. "almah") will conceive. When she is giving birth to a son, she will call his name Immanuel. (Isaiah 7:14 TLV)

"Joseph son of David, do not be afraid to take Miriam as your wife, for the Child conceived in her is from the Holy Spirit (Ruach ha-Kodesh). 21 She will give birth to a son; and you shall call His name Yeshua, for He will save His people from their sins." 22 Now all this took place to fulfill what was spoken by Adonai through the prophet, saying, 23 "Behold, the virgin shall conceive and give birth to a son, and they shall call His name Immanuel," which means "God with us." (Matt 1:20 TLV)

Satan used Adam and Eve to try and kill God as He was going to become the First Born of the New Creature. To dwell with man and man with God (as man). But God is God and Satan failed.

Eve's First Pregnancy

A good question was raised when discussing this theory, that of Eve being pregnant before she and Adam had sex the first time. That part of their relationship took place after the fall, outside of Eden. Was Eve pregnant while still in Eden? The core of this entire thesis rests on this being the case, that Eve was a virgin, pregnant with Immanuel, "God with us" as described earlier.

The end of Genesis 3 states they are driven out of Eden.

> *therefore the Lord God sent him out from the garden of Eden, to cultivate the ground from which he was taken. 24 So He drove the man out; and at the east of the garden of Eden He stationed the cherubim and the flaming sword which turned every direction to guard the way to the tree of life. (Gen 3:23 NASB)*

Then in Genesis 4 they "know" each other.

Now the man had relations with his wife Eve, and she conceived and gave birth to Cain, (Gen 4:1 NASB)

It is shown they did not have sex until after being driven out of Eden and thereby conceiving their first child together.

The comment that nowhere does it say Eve was pregnant when in the Garden is true. It's a valid point. The Bible does not specifically say that. The Bible also does not specifically say what they did either. It uses metaphors, analogies, and vague references. It is definitely difficult, if not heretical to say something is stated in the Bible when it is not already obviously, clearly and specifically stated. So, the use of interpretation of the Bible's many nuances, metaphors, analogies and patterns must be used to carefully put the various pieces together.

A very poetic metaphor or analogy of conception can be seen in the very beginning of Genesis.

> The earth was formless and void, and darkness was over the surface of the deep, and the Spirit of God was moving over the surface of the waters. 3 Then God said, "Let there be light"; and there was light. 4 God saw that the light was good; and God separated the light from the darkness. (Gen 1: 2 NASB)

The entire description of the first day through the second could almost be describing the beginning moments of the conception of a child deep in the mother's womb. The child as yet being without form and void, in the darkness, in the waters. The Holy Spirit hovering over the waters is similar to what is stated in the gospel of Luke.

> The angel answered and said to her, "The Holy Spirit will come upon you, and the power of the Most High will overshadow you; and for that reason the holy Child

shall be called the Son of God. (Luke 1:35 NASB)

Then God creates the light of life.

In the beginning was the Word, and the Word was with God, and the Word was God. 2 He was in the beginning with God. 3 All things came into being through Him, and apart from Him nothing came into being that has come into being. 4 In Him was life, and the life was the Light of men. 5 The Light shines in the darkness, and the darkness did not comprehend it.(John 1:1 NASB)

In the beginning was the Word. The Word was with God, and the Word was God. 2 He was with God in the beginning. 3 All things were made through Him, and apart from Him nothing was made that has come into being. 4 In Him was life, and the life was the light of men. 5 The light shines in the darkness, and the darkness has not overpowered it. (John 1:1 TLV)

These quotes are the same passage from two different translations. They are almost identical except for the last phrase. The reference to how the light and darkness are compared. This will be discussed shortly.

The question of whether the Bible says something specifically stated or not, is not as strong an argument as it may seem in this case. The Bible does not say specifically in Genesis that Messiah is there at the beginning. That fact can only be gleaned from the statement "and God Said". Only when one realizes Messiah is the Word of God, is therefore the spoken Word of God which caused creation to come into being. It is only then Messiah is understood to be there at creation. The Bible does not specifically state Messiah is there.

In short, we have to infer Messiah was there through the implications of the statement "and God said". John clarifies this in the opening statements in his gospel.

So how do we see if something which isn't specifically stated is actually there? By using other passages of the Bible, just as we do when reading John 1, and comparing it to Genesis 1.

A number of these passages have already been quoted previously but here are a few to help make the case that, even though the Bible does not specifically state Eve was pregnant before she knew Adam, never the less, she was going to give birth. A virgin birth just as Miriam eventually did.

> *He is the image of the invisible God, the firstborn of all creation. (Col 1: 15 TLV)*

> *"Before I formed you in the womb I knew you, and before you were born I consecrated you; (Jeremiah 1:5 NASB)*

> *Therefore the Lord Himself will give you a sign: Behold, a virgin will be with child and bear a son, and she will call His name Immanuel. (Isaiah 7:14 NASB)*

*"Before she travailed, she brought forth;
Before her pain came, she gave birth to a
boy. 8 "Who has heard such a thing? Who
has seen such things? (Isaiah 66: 7 NASB)*

Throughout the Bible the Messiah is repeatedly

referred to as the Lamb of God, a baby.

*Like a lamb that is led to slaughter, And
like a sheep that is silent before its
shearers, (Isaiah 53:7 NASB)*

*The next day he *saw Jesus coming to him
and *said, "Behold, the Lamb of God who
takes away the sin of the world! (John
1:29NASB)*

*and he looked at Jesus as He walked, and
*said, "Behold, the Lamb of God!" (John
1:36 NASB)*

*but with precious blood, as of a lamb
unblemished and spotless, the blood of
Christ. (1Peter 1:19NASB)*

Look at the statement concerning Miriam and

compare her to Eve.

when His mother Mary had been betrothed to Joseph, before they came together she was found to be with child by the Holy Spirit. (Matthew 1: 18 NASB)

Until finally it is clarified He was slain from the foundations of the world. At the time period of Creation.

And all that dwell upon the earth shall worship him, whose names are not written in the book of life of the Lamb slain from the foundation of the world. (Rev 13:8 KJV)

So, yes, it is not specifically stated in Genesis that Eve was pregnant before she knew Adam. That can only be surmised by examining the rest of the Scriptures and by putting all the pieces together.

The Bible does not specifically say a virgin either, the word used (almah עַלְמָה) which inherently implies it will be a virgin. The word itself refers to that of a young woman, one who has not as yet been married, therefore a virgin. Some things need to be discerned by the reader through further study, investigation, and analysis.

Going back to the comparison of the two versions of John. In the first the darkness did not "comprehend", whereas in the second the darkness did not "overpower" the light. Using both words, the child inside the mother, in this case Eve, the "darkness" was unable to understand or defeat the child, the Messiah at this point. If this thesis is correct, then this could imply the Adversary could not understand the greater implications of the forthcoming child and at that moment was unable to stop it. It wasn't until the time of the birth would the child become vulnerable. Once born, the parents would instinctually care for and protect it. Satan had to act fast and cause them to succumb before the parents do what they're supposed to.

A lot of this goes directly to comparing Eve to Miriam, one sinned, one did not. The one who did not sin gave birth. The one who did sin must have done something which would be the polar opposite.

One final woman of Jewish antiquity. The one of legend.

Lilith

The story or legend of Lilith is an interesting one. It seems to center primarily on dominance of one gender over the other and aspects of sexuality. These aspects of the legend of Lilith are not germane to this discussion. The story or stories go into details which are in some cases wild speculation and obvious mythology and legend. It must also be emphasized it is a legend comprised from speculations and good story telling, including rather salacious aspects

The most familiar writings of Lilith come from the near east somewhere between the 8th and 10th centuries CE. However, there are far more ancient versions relating to the same idea dating to some 3000 BCE. There are also references to her in the Talmud and other Jewish writings.

The main point of these stories and the reason they are included in this commentary is, Lilith is according to these legends, the first wife of Adam, preceding Eve. There is one author who attributes the two women, Lilith and Eve to actually be the same individual. My contention is this latter idea would be the more accurate one if it were true.

Contained within the legend of Lilith is her rebuking of God's commands, she is then cursed to supply one hundred of her dead children as a kind of atonement. Another part of her defiance is that of Adam as the one to rule over her.

According to the legend, related to the aspect of her supplying so many of her own dead children is her dominance over male children for the first eight days of their life. This kind of shows how it's a legend which developed later as it's not until Abraham that God commands all the male children to be circumcised.

Within another aspect of the legends of Lilith is how she, as a demonic figure is the alleged reason for crib deaths or "Sudden Death Syndrome". The point here being, the first "wife" of Adam is through legend responsible for the death of children. It is said there is always a kernel of truth behind every legend.

I do not believe or suggest Adam had a first wife. The first woman was not as yet named. That didn't happen until after sin had entered the world. The authors of the Lilith legends were somehow touching on the reality of what actually happened and penned their various stories that oddly and accurately fit this scenario. The first woman was or is somehow connected to the death of a child and children, even to the moment of birth. This is precisely the point of this entire discussion and the reason the story is mentioned.

It may be these stories are a way of separating the goodness envisioned in Eve as the first woman from the evil which the as yet unnamed woman with Adam committed. In other words, Lilith is a pseudonym for Eve before the fall. In this case I am in agreement with the one author who does suggest they are the same person.

Again, this is not Biblical. It is a legend thousands of years old from the ancient near east. It is included to show how in the mind of Jewish and other ancient cultures, the thought already existed of the first woman having infant deaths attributed to her.

The Stranger in Your Midst

One point to make is the continuing theme of loving the stranger or your neighbor. This is another of the many themes, types, and patters in the Bible. It is a well-known tradition throughout the near and middle east, to care for and protect the visitor, guest or stranger who may come to you at any given time.

In truth even your neighbor is a stranger in your midst. Do any of us really know one another? How often have we heard testimonies from people about how they "thought" they knew their neighbor and found it difficult to understand why or how that person did something?

We can see in the following passages the repeating emphasis on loving one's neighbor and the stranger in our midst, "among us".

You shall not take vengeance, nor bear any grudge against the sons of your people, but you shall love your neighbor as yourself; I am the Lord. (Lev 19:18 NASB)

'And if a stranger dwell with you in your land, you shall not mistreat him. 34 The stranger who dwells among you shall be to you as one born among you, and you shall love him as yourself; (Lev 19:33 KJV)

Notice in the previous passage the direct correlation to "**one born among you, and you shall love him as yourself**".

Therefore love the stranger, for you were strangers in the land of Egypt. (Deut 10:19 KJV)

And he said unto him, Thou shalt love the Lord thy God with all thy heart, and with all thy soul, and with all thy mind. 38 This is the great and first commandment. (Matthew 22:37 ASV)

Jesus answered, the first is, Hear, O Israel; The Lord our God, the Lord is one:

30 and thou shalt love the Lord thy God with all thy heart, and with all thy soul, and with all thy mind, and with all thy strength. 31 The second is this, Thou shalt love thy neighbor as thyself. There is none other commandment greater than these. (Mark 12:29 ASV)

A newborn child is still a stranger, even to the parents. The child is a new individual to meet and learn about. True the child must be properly taught and raised, but in all that process the child will still grow up to be their own person, an individual.

Then Messiah bringing proper understanding of the Scriptures made a clarification of the concept of the neighbor in relation to the "stranger in your midst".

And behold, a certain lawyer stood up and made trial of him, saying, Teacher, what shall I do to inherit eternal life? 26 And he said unto him, what is written in the law? how readest thou? 27 And he answering said, Thou shalt love the Lord thy God with all thy heart, and with all thy soul, and with all thy strength, and with all thy mind; and thy neighbor as thyself. 28 And he said unto him, Thou hast answered right: this do, and thou shalt live. 29 But he, desiring to justify himself, said unto Jesus, And who is my neighbor? 30 Jesus made answer and said, A certain man was going down from Jerusalem to Jericho; and he fell among robbers, who both stripped him and beat him, and departed, leaving him half dead. 31 And by chance a certain priest was going down that way: and when he saw him, he passed by on the other side. 32 And in like manner a Levite also, when he came to the place, and saw him, passed by on the other side. 33 But a certain Samaritan, as he journeyed, came where he was: and when he saw him, he was moved with compassion, 34 and came to him, and bound up his wounds, pouring on them oil and wine; and he set him on his own beast, and brought him to an inn, and took care of him. 35 And on the morrow he took out two shillings, and gave them to the host, and said, Take care of him; and whatsoever thou spendest more, I, when I come back again, will repay thee. 36 Which of these three,

thinkest thou, proved neighbor unto him
that fell among the robbers? 37 And he
said, He that showed mercy on him. And
Jesus said unto him, Go, and do thou
likewise. (Luke 10:25 ASV)

This command to love your neighbor was and is potentially foreshadowed by what happened in Eden. They did not love or care for the new "stranger in their midst". A lesson which later needed to be codified for the rest of humanity. Sorry to say we have not quite learned that lesson yet even after thousands of years.

This parable teaches not only the need for the willingness to love the stranger and help one another. It also teaches the stranger and the neighbor are basically one and the same. All are neighbors and strangers, all should be loved accordingly.

As just mentioned, this would have been violated in Eden as the newborn child, ostensibly a stranger in their midst, was not welcomed, cared for and loved. Exactly the opposite took place. Evil befell the two people and subsequently the child was murdered.

Lastly, you do not know who that stranger is.

> *Forget not to show love unto strangers: for thereby some have entertained angels unawares. (Heb 13:2 ASV)*

Mentioned earlier is the use of the phrase "The angel of the Lord". That the term represents the pre-incarnate Messiah Yeshua. We never know who the stranger is. Even Yeshua was unrecognized by two of His disciples on the road to Emmaus.

> *And behold, two of them were going that very day to a village named Emmaus, which was about seven miles from Jerusalem. 14 And they were talking with each other about all these things which*

had taken place. 15 While they were talking and discussing, Jesus Himself approached and began traveling with them. 16 But their eyes were prevented from recognizing Him.   (Luke 24:13 NASB)

Could that passage be a reflection of Eden? Two people were unaware of the presence of the Son of God who then proceeded to teach them knowledge about the Scriptures. Does this reflect how Adam and Eve did not know the new stranger? There were no midwives, no "neo-natal" care or emergency care centers.   There wasn't even another woman who had been pregnant to tell her what was happening or what to do. And so, she followed the advice of the Adversary.

The Abomination of Desolation.

The Abomination of Desolation שִׁקּוּצִים מְשֹׁמֵם.

Doing something so hateful it leaves someone or something completely empty. The feeling of being empty, desolate brings up the next major point. The phrase is first used in the book of Daniel. This is a very important phrase in Bible interpretation and prophecy.

> and on the wing of <u>abominations</u> will come one who makes desolate, even until a complete destruction, one that is decreed, is poured out on the one who makes <u>desolate</u>." (Daniel 9:27 NASB)

שִׁקּוּצִים מְשֹׁמֵם

So here is a combination of thoughts on this term.

Abomination שִׁקּוּצִים "Shiqquts"

abomi·na·tion (ə bäm'ə nā'shən)

noun

1. an abominating; great hatred and disgust; loathing

2. anything hateful and disgusting.

When looking at the word pictures of the Ancient Hebrew letters we see a picture form for these words.

Shiqquts is the Hebrew word for abomination, it is made of the Hebrew letters "sheen", "kuf", "vav" and "tsade". Shiqquts is the Hebrew word used for something which is impure or detestable.

שִׁקּוּץ

שׁ Sheen is represented by teeth and means to consume or destroy שׁ

ק Qoof represents the back of the head and means "behind", the last, the least. ק

ו Vav represents a hook, spike, peg or nail and

represent those or mean "and", to add, to secure ו

צ Tsade represents a fishhook and means to catch,

harvest, desire, need. צ

שִׁקּוּץ

In the word shiqquts, the teeth destroy and

consume. What is it that it consumes? The vav connects

(and or adds together) the two words for the back of the

head and the fishhook. A pretty gruesome thought. A nail

and fishhook to the back of a head? Is this word as it is

spelled in the Hebrew, suggesting that which is consumed

and destroyed comes as a result of a nail or hook to

someone's head? (A very good description of partial birth

abortion.) Something to consider is the first two letters,

"sheen & qoof" which make up the word translated as

"sack". Is this also a reference to an "amniotic" sack of a newborn child?

Desolation שָׁמֵם "shameem"

deso·la·tion (des′ə lā′shən)

noun

1. a making desolate; laying waste.

2. a desolate condition

3. lonely grief; misery

4. loneliness

5. a desolate place

    The word for "desolation" is "shamem" and is

    comprised of the letters Sheen, Mem & Mem

    שָׁמֵם

    שׁ Sheen is represented by teeth and means to consume

or destroy שׁ

מַ Mem represents water, liquid which can be calm or chaotic. מ

מ Mem represents water, liquid which can be calm or chaotic. מ

שָׁמֵם

The word pictures in shamem show an all-consuming devastation involving water. The cleansing actions of chaotic waters as they wash over all in its path. The repetition of the "mem" is an emphasis on the symbolism of the strength of the chaos of the waters. One can see a simple and direct comparison to Noah and the flood as those waters washed over the earth; washing away the abominations taking place at that time.

In the context of this thesis, a comparison can be made of the water breaking at the birth of a child. Combine that with the hook and back of the head and we have the gruesome sight of the brain fluids and blood, which look like a mix of water and blood. The same image which can be seen when Messiah's side was pierced with the spear. The same imagery of the blood and water being washed out of the side of the Temple during the sacrifice.

After the commission of the deed in Eden a short trial took place, God inquired of the serpent, Adam, and Eve of what had happened. God already knew the answers, but justice requires the accused to have a chance to respond to the accusations and possibly refute any allegations or facts.

God is a righteous judge! After the trial, the judgment was imposed, and a probationary time set. The time of that probation would show if the judgment was truly just and righteous. It also shows God's love and compassion as it gives the accused a chance to redeem his or herself. However, a probationary period is not open ended. It will one day come to a closure. God's appointed time of the imposition of the penalty of death will eventually come at His discretion. This death penalty, this execution of judgment, of the criminal(s) did happen and was fulfilled on the Cross or Execution Stake by Yeshua.

Sadly, mankind during this probationary period demonstrates time and time again he is incapable of living righteously according to his own will and needs to live by the Will of God; have the Spirit (Ruach) of God installed in his heart, replacing his own selfish heart of stone.

The Abomination of Desolation as spoken of by the prophets is not just the idea of a statue being built, or just of some man wanting to be God. It's the age-old curse against man himself. In Eden the temptation wasn't just food, Adam and Eve were tempted to be elevated to the same level as God. Is this not what the theologians have been saying someone will one day arise and proclaim? The

Abomination of Desolation the "shiqqutsim mashamem"

$$\text{שִׁקּוּצִים מְשֹׁמֵם}$$

is man making himself as God. Adam and Eve

were actually the first to commit this act, the Abomination

of Desolation as they attempted to make themselves like

God.

Once again, the Book of Daniel.

> *And from the time that the continual*
> *burnt-offering shall be taken away, and*
> *<u>the abomination that maketh desolate</u> set*
> *up, there shall be a thousand two hundred*
> *and ninety days. (Daniel 12:11 ASV*
> *emphasis mine)*

Some have theorized it merely refers to a person

who exalts them self as God. This may be true but could be

only true in part. It may not just be a statue in particular. It is more the act of a man trying to be "god". Some liken the statue in Daniel and the statue erected to Molech in Jerusalem which then had babies sacrificed to it. It isn't so much the graven image, a definite sin as seen in the book of Exodus (20), but the horrific slaying of the children.

Yeshua refers to this when He warns His followers of things to come. It is interesting to note the inclusion of the warning against women who are pregnant or are nursing babies.

> *"Therefore when you see the <u>abomination of desolation</u> which was spoken of through Daniel the prophet, standing in the holy place (let the reader understand), 16 then those who are in Judea must flee to the mountains. 17 Whoever is on the housetop must not go down to get the things out that are in his house. 18 Whoever is in the field must not turn back to get his cloak. 19 But woe to those who are pregnant and to those who are nursing babies in those days! (Matthew 24:15 NASB)*

The children were sacrificed for the betterment of the lives of the parents. Whether it was for immediate food or, so they would have a good year, good harvests, fortune and so on the end results were and are the same. This is the Original Sin of Adam and Eve. They were tempted to elevate themselves to a god like level, but in the process, they needed to murder the child being born.

The main point here is, it is not the action of the making of a statue, or of just someone wanting and trying to be God or be like God. Kings and emperors have done that for millennia with no abnormal results. So, there must be more to it.

It's more than the attempt by man to elevate himself to that of a god. It is the reenactment of Original Sin, the repeating of the assault on the FIRST BORN. A direct attack on God and the child. In essence the murder of the innocence.

The Biblical pattern of self-exalted kings begin with King Nimrod in Babylon and the tower. He tries in vain to elevate his position and existence to that of God. Later Pharaoh takes it further, then Antiochus Epiphanes, later Herod the Great, then the Roman Empire as well as all the other governments who one by one set themselves up in place of God. We are to be ruled over by God, not man. This is shown in the book of 1 Samuel.

> Then Adonai said to Samuel, "Listen to the voice of the people in all that they say to you. For they have not rejected you, rather they have rejected Me from being king over them. 8 Like all the deeds that they have done since the day I brought them out of Egypt to this day—forsaking Me and worshiping other gods—so they are doing to you also. 9 So now, listen to their voice. However, you must earnestly forewarn them, and declare to them the rulings of the king who will reign over them."

10 Now Samuel reported all the words of Adonai to the people who were asking him for a king. 11 "This will be the practice of the king that will reign over you," he said. "He will draft your sons and assign them as his charioteers and horsemen, and they will run before his chariots. 12 He will appoint them as commanders of thousands and captains of fifties, also some to plow his fields, reap his harvest, make his weapons of war and the equipment for his chariots. 13 Also he will take your daughters to be perfumers, cooks and bakers. 14 He will seize the best of your fields, vineyards and olive groves, and give them to his courtiers. 15 He will take a tenth of your grain and your vintage and give it to his officials and slaves. 16 He will also take your male and female servants, your best young men and your donkeys and make them do his work. 17 He will also take the tenth of your flocks. Then you yourselves will become his slaves. 18 When the day comes and you cry out because of your king, whom you have chosen for yourselves, Adonai will not answer you on that day." (1Samuel 8: 7 TLV)

Just as in Eden when Eve turned away from God as the source of direction and ruler ship, so too the Israelites turned from God. They demanded and earthly ruler.

Now a statue by itself is not an abomination of desolation; even though worshiping it is against God's Commandment it still does not reach the description of an "abomination of desolation" as described previously. Nor is a king thinking himself to be a god. That characteristic seems to be a prerequisite for the job.

What does rise to that level Biblically as well as instinctually? The killing of the children, the slaying of the first born, unborn, newborn, or fully born, the hated disgusting act which causes "loneliness," "laying waste", "making desolate", "emptiness". Sacrificing them on or to an idol would be an obvious part of that description.

The original and first Abomination of Desolation was the slaying of the children, murdering the innocent for no other reason than the convenience and comfort of the parents. Any excuse sufficed, any evil can be rationalized away when we lie to ourselves and abandon rationality.

One last point on the Abomination of Desolation. The word for desolation "shamem" שָׁמֵם is almost identical to the word for "heavens".שָׁמַיִם "shamaeem". There is only one difference, the absence of the letter "yud" י. The word for Desolation does not have this letter.

Ancient rabbinical thought posed this letter represents the Mashiach / Messiah. Similar to the word "Elohim" אֱלֹהִים a word used for God where in the middle letter is the letter Yud י. Messiah is in the word as a part of God, Elohim. This is not a "New Testament" or "Christian" idea or concept

The word "Desolation" is missing the Mashiach, the Son of God. The Son is missing. In the word for desolation, emptiness, the one letter representing the

Messiah is absent; it is empty. The Son of God has been

removed. In the word for "heavens" the Mashiach is there.

This situation can easily fit the prophetic aspect as well as

that which fits the point of this thesis.

Passing through the fire

"Passing through the fire." This phrase refers to the sacrifice of the baby to a god whose adherents believed it to have desired such a sacrifice for its favor. This would most notably be the first born but was not limited to having to be the first born. The action was to get favor from "the god(s)" for a good life, prosperity, a good harvest and similar blessings. Below is a list of passages which speak directly to this practice.

The Bible mentions this practice in the books of 1 & 2 Kings. The bible also mentions child sacrifice to other unnamed idols and gods of ancient Canaan. Other books of the Bible such as Psalms, Jeremiah and Ezekiel also speak of sacrificing children.

> *You shall not give any of your offspring to offer them to Molech, nor shall you*

profane the name of your God; I am the Lord. (Leviticus 18:21 NASB)

There shall not be found among you anyone who makes his son or his daughter pass through the fire, (Deuteronomy 18:10 NASB)

But he walked in the way of the kings of Israel, and even made his son pass through the fire, according to the abominations of the nations whom the Lord had driven out from before the sons of Israel. (2Kings 16:3 NASB)

Note the use of the word abomination and how they were driven out of the land.

Then they made their sons and their daughters pass through the fire, and practiced divination and enchantments, and sold themselves to do evil in the sight of the Lord, provoking Him. 18 So the Lord was very angry with Israel and removed them from His sight; none was left except the tribe of Judah. (2 Kings 17:17 NASB)

Again, the sacrifice of the children, something which was previously called an "abomination" is punished by driving the people from the land.

> *He made his son pass through the fire, practiced witchcraft and used divination, and dealt with mediums and spiritists. He did much evil in the sight of the Lord provoking Him to anger. 2Kings 21:6 NASB*

> *He also defiled Topheth, which is in the valley of the son of Hinnom, that no man might make his son or his daughter pass through the fire for Molech. (2 Kings 23:10 NASB)*

> *He made his sons pass through the fire in the valley of Ben-hinnom; and he practiced witchcraft, used divination, practiced sorcery and dealt with mediums and spiritists. He did much evil in the sight of the Lord, provoking Him to anger. (2 Chronicles 33:6 NASB)*

Molech is typically depicted as a bronze statue which is then heated with fire until the metal is glowing hot. In some cases, it has hands and arms in front on which the baby to be sacrificed is laid. The arms would raise, and the baby roll down into the heated belly of the idol.

They even sacrificed their sons and their daughters to demons. 38 They shed innocent blood—the blood of their sons and their daughters, sacrificed to the idols of Canaan. So, the land was desecrated with blood. 39 So they defiled themselves by their deeds and prostituted themselves by their practices. 40 Therefore the anger of Adonai was kindled against His people, and He abhorred His inheritance. (Psalms 106:37 TLV)

"The children of Judah have done what is evil in My sight"—it is a declaration of Adonai—"They have set their detestable things in the House that bears My Name to defile it. 31 They have built the high places of Topheth in the Valley of Ben-Hinnom to burn their sons and their daughters in the fire—which I did not command, nor did it even enter My mind. (Jer 7:30 TLV)

They have built high places for Baal, in order to burn their children in the fire as burnt offerings to Baal—something I never commanded, nor mentioned, nor did it ever come into My mind.'" (Jer 19:5 TLV)

They built the high places of Baal in the Valley of Ben-Hinnom, to make their sons and their daughters pass through fire to Molech—something I never commanded them, nor did it enter My mind that they would do this loathsome thing, causing Judah to sin." (Jer 32:35 TLV)

"You took your sons and your daughters whom you bore for Me, and sacrificed them to be eaten by them. Were your obscene practices not enough? 21 You slaughtered My children, making them pass through fire for them. 22 In all your abominations and harlotry, you have not remembered the days of your youth, when you were naked and bare, kicking about in your blood. (Ezekiel 16:20 TLV)

I let them become polluted in their own gifts, when <u>they offered up all that opened the womb to pass through the fire, so that I might make them desolate</u>, so that they would know that I am Adonai. (Ezekiel 20:26 TLV)

Note how in the passage above Ezekiel connects the womb, the abominable act and desolation.

> Therefore say to the house of Israel, thus says Adonai Elohim: Will you pollute yourselves after the manner of your fathers and go after their abominations? 31 When offering your gifts, making your sons pass through the fire, you keep polluting yourselves with all your idols, up to this day. (Ezekiel 20:30 TLV)

> For they have committed adultery and blood is on their hands. They have committed adultery with their idols and even _offered their children, whom they bore for Me, to be devoured._ (Ezekiel 23:37 TLV)

> On the same day that they slaughtered their children to their idols, they came into My Sanctuary to profane it. See, that is what they have done within My House! (Ezekiel 23:39 TLV)

Ezekiel repeatedly connects the sacrifice of children not only to the concept of an abomination but also that of desolation.

As the babies were being burned alive, the people would have drums and other instruments sounding as loudly as possible to drown out the screams and cries of the innocents as they burned to death.

Is it really so different today as the baby is ripped from the mother's womb and cut into pieces for sale? Even worse the partial birth when just as the baby is born the spinal column is severed and the skull is then pierced, and the brain is vacuumed out? A true abomination. The sacrifice of children on Temple Mount happened, it's the "Abomination of Desolation".

> *On the same day that they slaughtered their children to their idols, they came into My Sanctuary to profane it. See, that is what they have done within My House! (Ezekiel 23:39 TLV)*

This always seemed to happen prior to the casting out of the people from the Land of Israel / Judaea. The pattern all started in Eden. Adam and Eve committed the act and were cast out of the land, "Eden". It is later replayed in the time of Noah when all the evil was swept away by the chaotic waters.

During the siege of Jerusalem in 70AD, Josephus tells us it happened again. Once again, the people were then "kicked out" of the land God had given them. The pattern is quite clear. This IS the Abomination of Desolation. When this happens, God will kick the people out of the land. Yeshua warned of this happening in Jerusalem before its destruction and warned His followers to leave the moment they saw it.

It is believed by some eschatology writers, this (the Abomination of Desolation) will happen once more before the arrival of the Messiah. This continual pattern points to only one conclusion; Original Sin consisted of Adam and Eve killing their first-born child, the First Born of Creation.

The serpent tempted Eve and thereby Adam, promising they would be as God.

The next Abomination of Desolation may very well be a man proclaiming himself as "God" or it may be mankind proclaiming itself as "God". The unbridled advancement of "science" may be the temptation. The human genetic manipulation or mutation researchers are toying with these very things today and this may very well allude to these actions.

This sounds a bit farfetched, but we see today how "modern man" self declares the god like ability with technology, weather, life and death (especially). We today allow for the slaying of the newborn and the unborn for no other reason than a convenience on the part of the mother. What may be worse is the ongoing sale of the body parts. Is there anything more disgusting and hateful, anything more an "Abomination"?

How hateful it must be to God to see a woman's womb made desolate. It is where He does His most amazing creative work, He creates a Man (or Woman). Original Sin is the original "Abomination of Desolation". An action so hateful and disgusting it causes not only a deep feeling of emptiness but a true emptiness. An emptiness like that of a mother in postpartum depression. An emptiness like one who cries for an only child. An emptiness of a land without its people. An emptiness of a people without their land.

Later in typical Biblical patterns, the action in Eden is played out again and again. Just prior to being driven out of the land, the people resort to cannibalism, (infantile cannibalism in particular). In Eden (Adam and Eve) committed the very first "Abomination" of "Desolation", something so hateful to God it caused Him to invoke the death penalty to His newly created creature "man". Then later removed the Man and Woman from the Garden created for them and God to dwell together in harmony. The pattern continues as was stated in Deuteronomy 28:4, the warning of disobedience.

Multiple times in the Scriptures God warns the people of the consequences of their disobedience. They would be driven from the land He gave them, just as Adam and Eve were driven out of the land God gave them.

The first time this happens is when Adam and Eve sin and they are driven from the land God has given them. Later during the time of Noah, the people are removed from the land due to their abominations. Then again in Sodom and Gomorrah the land is emptied and made desolate.

The pattern begins to become more focused and obvious during the time of the Israelites when they are driven from Egypt.

"Speak to the Children of Israel and say to them: I am Adonai your God. 3 You are not to act as they do in the land of Egypt, where you used to live. (Lev 18:9 TLV)

During that time as it is written, there was an edict to kill all the first-born male children which prompted the mother of Moses to cast him off in the Nile to spare his life. This was not the initial instigator of the removal of the Israelites from the land.

We see later when the subsequent Pharaoh then condemns the first born of Israel to death which itself prompts God to return the curse on the Egyptians. This may be a shadow of Eden but is not what instigates the removal of the Israelites from the land. Though they were in an oppressive servitude they were not as eager to leave as movies depict. Later in the wilderness they complained about how much better they were living in Egypt with sufficient food and accommodations.

What the Scriptures depict though is a slightly different scenario. God was giving them the land of Canaan. The land which God had promised Abraham, Isaac and Jacob. They were to drive out the Canaanites, putting everything to the sword sparing nothing. Why would God command such a thing? Look at what else is written about the land of Canaan and the Israelites.

> *You are not to act as they do in the land of Egypt, where you used to live. Nor are you to act as they do in the land of Canaan, where I am bringing you, nor are you to walk in their customs. 4 You are to obey My ordinances and keep My statutes and walk in them—I am Adonai your God. 5 So you are to keep My statutes and My ordinances. The one who does them will live by them. I am Adonai. (Lev 18:3 TLV)*

"When you come into the land which the Lord your God is giving you, you shall not learn to follow the abominations of those nations. 10 There shall not be found among you anyone who makes his son or his daughter pass through the fire, (Deut 18: 9 TLV.)

They were sacrificing the children to Molech. They were committing the Abomination of Desolation. It may be a fine though definite line between murdering someone else's children for your political purposes and murdering your own child or children for your own comfort. The point here being the Canaanites were committing the Abomination of Desolation and are then removed from the land as per God's direction to the Israelites.

The First Temple and subsequent dispersion.

Here are the quotations which speak of this pattern of history repeating itself in Jerusalem just prior to the people of God being removed from the land given them.

See, O Lord, and look! With whom have You dealt thus? Should women eat their offspring, the little ones who were born healthy? Lamentations (2:20NASB)

The hands of compassionate women boiled their own children; They became food for them (Lamentations 4:10 NASB).

Therefore, fathers will eat their sons among you, and sons will eat their fathers; for I will execute judgments on you and scatter all your remnant to every wind. (Ezekiel 5:10 NASB)

Here again, the punishment for this crime is to be driven from the land. A clear pattern exists of this crime and later to be driven out of the land.

And the king said to her, "What is the matter with you?" And she answered, "This woman said to me, 'Give your son that we may eat him today, and we will eat my son tomorrow.' 29 So we boiled my son and ate him; and I said to her on the next day, 'Give your son, that we may eat him'; but she has hidden her son." (Kings 6:28 NASB)

They slice off what is on the right hand but still are hungry, and they eat what is on the left hand but they are not satisfied; Each of them eats the flesh of his own arm. (Isaiah 9:20 NASB)

Another translation puts it this way:

One grabs with the right hand but is hungry, and eats with the left hand but is not satisfied. Everyone will eat the flesh of his own arm 20 Manasseh will devour Ephraim, and Ephraim, Manasseh, both are against Judah. (Isaiah 9:19 TLV)

"You who hate good and love evil, who tear off their skin from them and their flesh from their bones, 3 who eat the flesh of my people, strip off their skin from them, break their bones and chop them up as for

the pot and as meat in a kettle." 4 Then they will cry out to the Lord, but He will not answer them. Instead, He will hide His face from them at that time because they have practiced evil deeds. (Micah 3:2 NASB)

<u>*I will make them eat the flesh of their sons and the flesh of their daughters,*</u> *and they will eat one another's flesh in the siege and in the distress with which their enemies and those who seek their life will distress them."' (Jer 19:9 NASB emphasis mine)*

All five poems in Lamentations agree the catastrophe of the destruction of Jerusalem is God's punishment for sin.

God again alludes to the sin in Eden by forcing them to the point of eating their young. This symbolizes sin, the sin which began in Eden. Just like in the wilderness where they were forced to eat the symbol of their sin, the golden calf which was ground up and put in their water.

The Second Temple and dispersion.

There were no "Biblical" writings following the destruction of the Second Temple which touch on this. However, we do have an outside source which tells of it. Josephus Flavius talks of the same thing happening prior to the fall of Jerusalem in 70 AD.

[201] There was a certain woman that dwelt beyond Jordan, her name was Mary; her father was Eleazar, of the village Bethezob, which signifies the house of Hyssop. She was eminent for her family and her wealth and had fled away to Jerusalem with the rest of the multitude and was with them besieged therein at this time. The other effects of this woman had been already seized upon, such I mean as she had brought with her out of Perea and removed to the city. What she had treasured up besides, as also what food

*she had contrived to save, had been also carried off by the rapacious guards, who came every day running into her house for that purpose. This put the poor woman into a very great passion, and by the frequent reproaches and imprecations she east at these rapacious villains, she had provoked them to anger against her; but none of them, either out of the indignation she had raised against herself, or out of commiseration of her case, would take away her life; and if she found any food, she perceived her labors were for others, and not for herself; and it was now become impossible for her any way to find any more food, while the famine pierced through her very bowels and marrow, when also her passion was fired to a degree beyond the famine itself; nor did she consult with anything but with her passion and the necessity she was in. She then attempted a most unnatural thing; and snatching up her son, who was a child sucking at her breast, she said, "**O thou miserable** __*infant!*__ *for whom shall I preserve thee in this war, this famine, and this sedition? As to the war with the Romans, if they preserve our lives, we must be slaves. This famine also will destroy us, even before that slavery comes upon us. Yet are these seditious rogues more terrible than both the other.* __**Come on; be thou my food,**__ *and be thou a fury to these seditious varlets, and a by-word to the world, which is all that is now wanting to complete the calamities of us Jews."* __**As soon as she had said this, she slew her son, and then roasted him, and eat the one half of him,**__ *and kept the other half by her concealed. Upon this the seditious came in presently, and smelling the horrid scent of this food, they threatened her that they would cut her throat immediately if she did not show them what food she had gotten ready. She replied that she had saved a very fine portion of it for them, and withal uncovered what was left of her son. Hereupon they were seized with a horror and* *amazement of mind, and stood astonished at the sight,*

when she said to them, "This is mine own son, and what

hath been done was mine own doing! Come, eat of this

food; for I have eaten of it myself! Do not you pretend to be

either more tender than a woman, or more compassionate

than a mother; but if you be so scrupulous, and do

abominate this my sacrifice, as I have eaten the one half,

let the rest be reserved for me also."

Flavius Josephus, The Wars of the Jews Book 6,

Ch3 Sec. 4, William Whiston, A.M., Ed.

The pattern is evident, repeat the sin of Eden and you're driven from the land He has given you. God warned of this repeatedly. It first happened in Eden, then again in Jerusalem around 600BC and again in 70AD. The reason was the same, the curse remained. Though this happened in Egypt around 1500 BC, it was not of their doing or sin.

That was just another reflection. At that time, it was the Canaanites, this showing anyone is susceptible to this punishment for this sin, the sin which started them all.

Each time God's people were driven from the land they inhabited, the murder of children was taking place. In some cases, it included the act of cannibalism. The Abomination of Desolation, that hateful thing which makes something empty.

Mom and Dad killed me.

With the image of a child reaching his arms up to his parents to be picked up, Messiah stretched out His arms and cried "Father, forgive them, they don't know what they are doing!".

He was asking for the forgiveness of His first set of parents, Adam and Eve and thereby of all mankind. The only reason He came and died was to atone for the sin of mankind, that which happened in Eden. True it included all the subsequent sins of mankind, but the primary reason began in Eden. The "Generational Curse" started by the actions in the Garden of Eden was broken at that moment.

When He cried from the cross "My God, my God why have you forsaken me?" it is the same as when he was murdered the first time, except now the price was being paid for their sin.

He was calling to the other two aspects of the Divinity. Such a triad can be seen in the famous prayer in Deuteronomy 6:4 known as the "Sh'ma" short for: "Sh'ma Y'israel, *Adonai*, Eluhanu, *Adonai* Echaad" which means "Hear, O Israel: The LORD our God, the LORD is one".

Note how God is referenced to three times in one verse: "**The Lord**, **Our God**, **The Lord**"; closing with "**is one**" or in Hebrew "echaad".

The Rambam (Maimonides) even noticed and noted the three-fold aspects of this important Hebrew prayer; although he did not at that time notice or comment on any possible significance of it.

We can get a better feel for the word echaad by briefly examining a couple of additional verses.

> *Therefore shall a man leave his father and his mother, and shall cleave unto his wife: and they shall be one (echaad) flesh. (Genesis 2:24 ASV)*

Regarding the people of the earth after the flood we read in

> *The Lord said, "Behold, they are one (echaad) people, (Genesis 11:6 NASB)*

He was the third part, the visible part of the invisible God crying out to the other two aspects of the Divinity.

Messiah was now crying out loud. He was no longer a baby "dumb before His shearer" and unable to speak.

When He cried "it is finished", He was as we know referring to the completion of God's plan to reconcile what happened in Eden, reconcile Himself with mankind. The punishment had been handed down, blood for blood. Everything Yeshua did was because of the actions of Adam and Eve in Eden.

Messiah took on Himself the sins of who were to be His parents, the parents of all mankind; and paid the death penalty they (and we) inherited. The probationary period had ended. This action restores humanity to the position God had intended. We fix our instinctual problem by choosing to live according to the Will of the Creator Father God.

Yeshua, the Messiah was as it says in Rev 13:8, ". . . the lamb who was slain from the creation of the world". This snippet would not be of such merit if so many other Biblical types and parallels did not support this position long before the book of Revelation.

This is a direct reference to Genesis; Yeshua was that lamb who was slain at the creation of the world. He was that child who reached up to His human (step) father and wondered silently why he was being betrayed and forsaken by him, just before His mother executed Him.

She violated her Feminine role to nurture and raise and develop the child, their future and the future of

Creation. She provided nourishment to Adam, usurping the role of God the Father. "Man does not live by bread alone, but by every word which proceeds from the mouth of God".

Like God as Father, the human father of the family is to provide the resources for food to the family. The mother then uses the resources and transforms it into food for the family. This can be seen as the woman transforms the seed of the man into another human being.

Finally, Satan ends up being cast into a spiritual prison. His plan of getting the Throne from God failed miserably. Instead of stopping God and preventing the creation to continue, God's creation continues and there are now billions of new souls of man, all with the power through faith to rebuke the Adversary.

Now compare this to what happened with Abraham and Isaac.

Abraham

Abraham, the great founding father of the faith, was promised by God that his seed would bless all nations. Of course, in the long run this referenced the coming of the Messiah.

God challenged Abraham with one specific test. He told him to take his promised son Isaac up to the mountain and sacrifice him. Abraham was aghast at this but, obeyed God. We see all kinds of prophetic references to the coming of the Messiah Yeshua. The cord of firewood laid on Isaac's shoulders shadowed the carrying of the Execution Stake. The ram which was sacrificed was caught in the thicket of thorns as Messiah was crowned with thorns.

How this relates to Original Sin is pretty obvious. God wanted to see if Abraham would actually kill his son for no other reason than he was instructed to by God. Would he obey God at all costs? At the same time, God was saying "NO!" to his killing of his son, teaching the killing of the child is wrong.

> Then they came to the place of which God had told him; and Abraham built the altar there and arranged the wood, and bound his son Isaac and laid him on the altar, on top of the wood. 10 Abraham stretched out his hand and took the knife to slay his son. 11 But the angel of the Lord called to him from heaven and said, "Abraham, Abraham!" And he said, "Here I am." 12 He said, "Do not stretch out your hand against the lad, and do nothing to him; for now I know that you fear God, since you have not withheld your son, your only son, from Me." (Genesis 22: 9 NASB)

God STOPS Abraham from killing his son to honor Him. This is diametrically opposed to what Molech's followers did. This entire incident was a test on multiple levels.

It was a test of Abraham's faith and trust of course.

It was a test to see if Abraham was worthy of the sacrifice

yet to come, the one who would remove the death penalty

man was deserving of through Adam. A Test to see if it

was still in man's heart and mind to kill one's child. This

was a test to see if Abraham (as kind of a representative of

man), would kill his child, for God. But we know from the

Scriptures God didn't want the child or children slain.

> *Therefore, just as sin came into the world through one man, and death through sin, and so death spread to all men because all sinned— 13 for sin indeed was in the world before the law was given, but sin is not counted where there is no law. 14 Yet death reigned from Adam to Moses, even over those whose sinning was not like the transgression of Adam, who was a type of the one who was to come.* (Romans 5:12 NASB)
>
> *For as by a man came death, by a man has come also the resurrection of the dead. 22 For as in Adam all die, so also in Messiah*

shall all be made alive. 1 (Corinthians 15:21 NASB)

Today, thousands of years later, as we proclaim our "modern civility", we murder the newborns by the thousands daily. For what reason? Some for personal convenience or because some "don't want to be a mother", they don't want the responsibility and the list goes on. We who are more "civilized" are just as blood thirsty as the ancients. With smug arrogance and ignorance, we do exactly what the ancients did.

Boiling a Kid in its Mother's Milk

While thinking about the clean food commands of the Torah, the oddity of the meat and dairy practices which are taught today caught my attention. Today, Rabbinic Judaism teaches against the mixing of meat and dairy. Whether it is actually together like the proverbial "cheeseburger" or merely cooked together or in the same pan or grill or whatever the method may be.; even if they had been cleaned beforehand. One is not even supposed to use the same utensils e.g. plates, forks, spoons etc.

Looking up where this stems from is a command first appearing in the book of Exodus

> *"You shall bring the choice first fruits of your soil into the house of the Lord your God. "You are not to boil a young goat in the milk of its mother. (Exodus 23:19 NASB)*

There is no mention of a prohibition against mixing meat and dairy. There is no mention of such anywhere in the entire Bible. As stated earlier, there are certain meats one is not to eat due to potential diseases and such, but nothing to do with mixing any of them with any kind of a dairy product. So where does this come from?

It may sound like a bizarre way to cook a young goat by today's standards. It was not the case thousands of years ago and cultures away from modern society.

The command is issued a few times in the Torah. First in Exodus 23, then in Exodus 34 and again in Deuteronomy 14

> *"You shall bring the very first of the first fruits of your soil into the house of the Lord your God. "You shall not boil a young goat in its mother's milk." (Exodus 34:26 NASB)*

You shall not boil a young goat in its mother's milk. Deut (14:21 NASB)

Why would God want to emphasize this one practice so much by stating it three times? It must be of such meaning and significance to God it had to be written in the Torah three times. There are a few opinions on this which are germane to this discussion.

The first is, it is believed at that time in that region the pagan cultures would boil the kid (young goat) in its mother's milk as part of a fertility rite. The liquid would then be sprinkled on the gardens, crops, fields, or orchards as a way of potentially improving their respective harvests.

According to Dr. Ralph Cudworth, FRS (1617 – 26 June 1688), It was customary during that period the people would boil the kid in the mother's milk and then use the broth in a fertility rite by sprinkling it on the trees, fields, and gardens.

This is really less related to their Kosher or food restrictions as much as it is with following pagan practices. However, I think there is more to this which is directly on point with this thesis.

A second point to this is made in connection to the instinctual and inherent relationship between a mother and her child. It is a major lesson hidden in a subtle way. What is not so subtle is it is mentioned multiple times, so it has definite significance. God is pointing out how profane it is to use the mother to be the source of death to the child. It violates in an almost cynical way the special relationship and bond a mother should have with her child or children.

It can be easily seen how this all relates to this theory of the original sin in Eden. The relationship between a mother and her child is depicted in a very profane way, specifically depicting the suckling young who is dead in its mother's milk.

An interesting point is how in the Exodus verse it places the command in relation to the appointed time of First Fruits. The Bible associates this practice specifically to the first of the three Biblical harvests, the harvest known as First Fruits. Once again, we see a direct Biblical connection of the mother, the death of the child and the reference to First Fruits.

Sin is Genetic

Adam and Eve at the fall caused the genetic corruption to start. *(Genesis, "become the descendants of Adam").* Genetics teaches us the human genome reproduces itself with a slow accumulation of defects which is then passed on to the next generation to add to. Thus, instead of "evolving" the human genome is actually "devolving".

Evil is the corruption entering an innocent world. Is there anything more evil than the decided act of killing one's child, even an unborn innocent child? This is stated with no apologies to the so called "prochoice" movement. The thrusting of an object of death into the innocent world of a child growing inside the mother's womb is part and parcel to the Original Sin of Adam and Eve in the Garden of Eden. It was at that moment mankind began to kill itself off starting with its own young. Just as Satan thrust Evil into the world, Adam and Eve thrust sin into humanity.

There is a much larger picture here, they, we, all of us inclusive, miss the realization of our place in relation to the Earth and life on a grand scale. It's our misconception that we are not a part of the entirety of the whole picture. It is our vanity that we own our bodies or our lives. We are just one breath away from losing it all. None of this is in our control.

then, after desire has conceived, it gives birth to sin; and sin, when it is full grown, gives birth to death" (James 1:15 TLV)

Cain and Able

To keep this idea going, look immediately at their family and in what manner it is dysfunctional. Remember the "Sin" on this level is inherited. The new first born (Cain), kills the second born (Abel). Anger, rage, jealousy, can anyone see anything good in those emotions? Cain's actions mimic the actions of his parents, only this time he asks the first question a man ever asks God. "Am I my brother's keeper?" This sets a lot of things in motion.

Then five generations later, Cain's descendent Lamech makes this comment:

> Lamech said to his wives, "Adah and Zillah, listen to my voice, you wives of Lamech, give heed to my speech, for I have killed a man for wounding me; and a boy for striking me; 24 If Cain is avenged sevenfold, then Lamech seventy-sevenfold." (Gen 4: 23 NASB)

This admission points directly to the continued sin of murder, the shedding of blood. The shedding of blood is the under pinning of the Judeo-Christian sin and redemption process. The penalty for murder is death. When the sin was committed in the Garden of Eden, man became mortal and would die; this also implies the entire species since they are the only two people at that time. God did not want to eradicate his new and favorite creature, "man"; even though man deserved it for his actions (similar to the serpent's) and brought it on himself.

Instead, God set in motion a plan and a system where His Creation could correct itself. Scripture is for correction as well as edification.

Could it be the moment a skewer of wood Eve or Adam used to penetrate the child and destroy God's plan is later reflected in the piercing the side of Messiah as BLOOD and WATER ran out? Does being nailed to the

Cross emphasize the piercings? What else would fit the scenario? Adam and Eve murdered their child, this very special and unique child as per Satan's direction. Though we ourselves are still liable for listening to him and not obeying God's Will; it's in our "DNA" at this point, the decisive will to disobey God's Will and try to do it our own. Only when we chose to do it His way through His Son is our spiritual (instinctual) DNA changed.

Is man worthy?

Consider the symbolism of leavening, yeast, the little bit that destroys the whole. The small action which contaminates or kills everything involved. This can be seen as symbolism of the tiny point of an object being stabbed through the cervix, uterus, embryo, killing the unborn child. It does not take much to kill a tiny child as any abortion clinic can readily attest.

Abraham is called forth to see if he'll obey God's Word, obey God's Will. That's the first test, does this creature God loves so much even have the ability in it to obey God's will? So, what does God tell him? He tells Abraham to kill his son! WHAT?! Well think about it. The action of killing your own child is going against God's Natural Law, the natural world needs to be corrected, but is the Human even still worth the effort?

Abraham is obedient as he ties down his son Isaac and is about to slay him. At the last moment God, sees Abraham is willingly obedient, hence "man", still has it within him to obey God's Will regardless of what it is. Now all that needs to be done is retrain him, "man". The virus patch to fix the programming that caused the evil choice is set in motion. The lineage of Abraham is started and promised in perpetuity. This is again antithetical of the action of an abortion by Adam and Eve.

Instead of killing Isaac, Abraham is given a goat to temporarily appease the need for the death penalty incurred by Adam. It's also the first step in a series of corrections to our thinking. Start with killing animals instead of people, (especially with the odd idea of your own child), use a lamb instead. God did not want to do away with His favorite whom He created with unbridled Love. That was Satan's design for God's Creation. Messiah Yeshua is God's total rebuke for the temptation of Eve and Original Sin.

For this <u>obedience</u> to God's will again, of not killing your child, (unborn or otherwise), life through the line of Abraham and thereby Yeshua will be kept for eternity. This would restore the original plan for man.

Look at some other clues to what the original sin was both symbolically and typologically.

Continuing with how "Sin" is in the genes.

It is significant the entire bible is based on these early passages of Genesis. These are all blatant arch types and symbols pointing directly backwards to the act of the abortion of a child in Eden.

In Genesis 4 God asks Cain where his brother is. With this vision in mind of the act of the parents, the question takes on an even deeper meaning. God, already knowing an older (step) brother was killed by Adam and

Eve, asks Cain if he even knows where his brother is. At the same time Cain has in his mind what he did to his own younger brother with the blood still on his hands. The sword of truth here is double edged in this question of man's next generation.

This is later born out again as Pontius Pilate tried in vain to wash his hands clean of the Messiah's blood, again signifying we all have the same "hereditary" sin of His blood on our hands but most significantly, this can only mean Adam and Eve have / had the same blood on their hands as well. The sin committed by Adam and Eve is in our genes.

How can that be unless, they aborted their first-born child and that can only be the First Born of Creation, Immanuel, "God With Us".

It also shows at the same time it is only through the shedding of the innocent blood we can wash our hands of

Original Sin. It was with blood the altar in the Temple was cleaned.

The test of Abraham and Isaac was to see whether or not Man should even be allowed to continue as a species; considering the actions of the ultimate parents Adam and Eve.

The sexual act isn't the sin, that act should be a beautiful thing between man and woman. What Adam and Eve did is the most evil of all acts a man and a woman can do, they deliberately murdered their child. Even worse, they ate remains of the child they murdered. They stopped the future.

The Bible is filled with reflections of what happened in Eden. These are the foreshadows of what will come. At the same time these may be the very reasons future events happened the way they did.

From Cain, the first to commit fratricide, through the times of Noah, Moses, the first siege of Jerusalem the incident in Eden, the sin is in the background. Then later with the arrival of Yeshua and his Last Supper, trial, and execution the events in Eden replay themselves. Lastly it was all repeated at the time of the second siege of Jerusalem as spoken of by Josephus. The sin of Adam and Eve is arguably still happening to this today.

Abraham and Isaac

As described earlier, Abraham was about to sacrifice Isaac, God through the Angel of the Lord stopped him at the last minute. God did not want Eden to be repeated. He clearly does not like the murdering of the children as has been shown. God stopped him and presented a goat caught in a thorn bush as a replacement sacrifice. This well-known foreshadow of the future Messiah, with the crown of thorns hinted of the lamb which would later be the final sacrifice for sin.

One of most glaring reflections or shadows of Eden comes up with what happened in Egypt.

Moses

When Moses was born it was during a time when the male children had come under a royal order of execution. All newborn male children were to be slain at birth. The mother of Moses saves the child who is then raised by Pharaoh's daughter. At the beginning the baby was cared for by his birth mother with the aid of his sister Miriam. Josephus describes the baby Moses as being so beautiful to look at people, would go out of their way to see him.

Pharaoh was given a challenge by God through Moses. It was Pharaoh's choice as to what the final catastrophic plague would be. What was Pharaoh's (evil) choice? <u>Kill the first born</u> of Israel. Again, we see the evil act of killing the child, the killing of the continuation of life, the ultimate evil. This shows up all over the Bible. Pharaoh too had in his heart the disobedience of God's Natural Will, as a result his firstborn was killed, and his line was ended. his family was made "desolate". Pharaoh and his firstborn, as well as the first born of all Egypt suffered the punishment for the murder of the children and at the same time stating the original crime of man, the firstborn child was killed.

To put the children of Israel under God's protection from the death penalty they were to slay a lamb and wipe its blood on the door posts and lintels of their homes and stay inside all evening, eating the cooked lamb until nothing was left.

These events are part of what is commonly known as the "Passover". In all this is where the symbol of the lamb is used specifically. Death passed over all who followed God's instructions. The final plague ended up being the death of the first born in Egypt. It was the first born of all present, even the livestock.

To spare themselves the Israelites were told to slay a lamb then paint its blood on the door posts and lintels of their homes. This would then protect them. This is seen as a foreshadow of the coming Messiah who would be the sacrificial lamb whose shed blood would protect and cleanse the world of sin. But there is another level to this which must be considered in light of this thesis.

Just as Adam and Eve would have been covered in the blood of the child, so too the Children of Israel were symbolically covered in blood by the spreading of the lamb's blood on their homes. The Blood of the Lamb was their "covering". This foreshadow is well known through the shed blood of Yeshua on the execution stake.

Going back to the word "adam" in Genesis, coincidentally, the second letter "dalet" ד represents a door. Now, due to the sin of Adam, covered in blood, it's now a door smeared with blood. Adam's blood stain shows up, hidden in the events in Egypt and the details of the Passover

In another parallel, just as Adam and Eve were covered in blood and were spared the death penalty, so too the Israelites were passed over by an immediate and impending death. Later they left, driven out of the land where they were living, similarly to Adam and Eve having been cast out of the garden. Every element of the last plague and the penalty of death passing over the Israelites reflects what took place in Eden.

> *Now Adonai had said to Moses, "I will bring one more plague upon Pharaoh and on Egypt. After that, he will let you go from here. When he lets you go, he will surely thrust you out altogether from here. (Exodus 11:1 TLV)*

These incidents play out on both levels representing the beginning and ending of sin. The sin which began in Eden. The sin takes place followed by the expulsion from the land.

This is all a reflection of Eden. The blood of the first born of creation was splattered all over Adam and Eve. In Egypt the blood of the lamb, in essence a child, was used as a marker for the repentant sinner and death passed by them. Just as the first created people, Adam and Eve were covered in blood but were spared the immediate death penalty for the slaying of the first born.

These symbols and motif continue through the rest of the Scriptures with the described sacrifices and events, ending with the sacrifice of the Messiah to remove the sin committed in Eden as well as the rest of the sins of mankind. (Ref: Isaiah 53) The trait we inherited from our original parents. The metaphor of the lamb compares the Messiah to that of an innocent baby. The reflection of Eden is in the child to be slain. Finally, when Yeshua entered Jerusalem for the last time the events in Eden began to replay themselves.

Yeshua's Birth

Once again, the foreshadow of Eden shows up. The child is born, and the adversary seeks to kill it. Just as Pharaoh sought to kill all the first-born males, now King Herod orders all the male children under 2 years of age to be slain.

> *Then when Herod saw that he had been tricked by the magi, he became furious. And he sent and killed all boys in Bethlehem and in all its surrounding area, from two years old and under, according to the time he had determined from the magi. (Matthew 2:16 TLV)*

The pattern has greater implications and support from other prophets of the Bible.

Consider the implications of this next verse. The Lord is saying how "they will look on ME whom they pierced...."

then they will look on Me whom they
pierced. Yes, they will mourn for Him as
one mourns for his only son, and grieve
for Him as one grieves for a firstborn. 11
In that day there shall be a great mourning
in Jerusalem, like the mourning at Hadad
Rimmon in the plain of Megiddo. 12 And
the land shall mourn, every family by
itself. (Zechariah 12:10 TLV.)

The comparison of the phrase "they will look <u>on</u> <u>me</u>", contrasts with "they will mourn <u>for him</u>". The two words "me" and "him". Clearly, it's referring to Messiah and the crucifixion, but is it only the crucifixion which is being referenced? The point being made is, not only is it referring to Messiah at His prophesied execution but is also pointing to the possibility of a slain child in Eden, the center point of the actions of Adam and Eve.

Scriptures tell us it's all about Messiah, beginning to end. Yeshua says they were written about Him.

You search the Scriptures because you
think that in them you have eternal life; it

is these that testify about Me; (John 5:39 NASB)

John emphasized this with the following statement.

For if you believed Moses, you would believe Me, for he wrote about Me. (John 5:46 NASB)

These passages are most definitively about Messiah. Will it be at the time of His return, the understanding of what took place will be evident? Will we finally know why Messiah had to come and do what He did; of how and why He saved mankind from the death penalty imposed in Eden.

Then, just as Adam and Eve realized at their sin, hiding in fear of the wrath of God, we too shall weep as one weeps for an only child. Knowing our own culpability for His death, our death. These verses would also be connecting the two, the crucified Messiah and the "lamb slain at the foundations of the earth" as being one and the same. The event in Eden, the action taken by Eve and

Adam was the slaying of the first born of Creation. The one who was never named. Never having survived long enough to be given a name.

He would have been at that time an only child, just as would be if this theory is accurate. There would have been only one child, the result of a virgin birth. The First Born of Creation as the Bible says. That child was then slain (at the foundations of the earth) by its parents after being tricked by the serpent. And so, realizing what they had done was horrifically wrong, they went and hid in fear.

We read in Jeremiah of the lamentation over the death of the children.

> *Thus says the Lord: "A voice was heard in Ramah, lamentation and bitter weeping, Rachel weeping for her children, refusing to be comforted for her children, because they are no more." (Jeremiah 31:15 TLV)*

There is a continuing theme throughout the Scriptures of the death of children. The sacrifice of Isaac which God halted at the last moment. The children of Israel under the edict of Pharaoh, then later the first born with the 10th plague. In the entire region there were children sacrificed to the various false gods and of course those slain under the order of Herod. The death of the child is a recurring theme. Is it so difficult to see how this could have been the beginning catalyst of all human sin as started in Eden? But there is another element to all this besides the slaying of the children.

Food

The dietary rules themselves are a reflection of Eden. God pointed to certain things which could be eaten for food, just as was done in Eden. In the process God specifically pointed to things which were not to be eaten.

Those things had the potential for disease, corruption and death. Again, just as in the garden.

Some creatures are for beauty, some are the world's garbage clean up creatures. Neither of these are to be eaten. We are not to eat the creatures for beauty and decoration or those which can be described as "the vacuum bag". Those are the creatures which are for cleaning up the garbage. You are what you eat. All this reflects Eden as the food God gives is replaced by foods we desire. Those we "think" we want or need. We end up getting the "fruits" of our desires.

In the wilderness God's people, the Israelites, were supplied with all they needed. They only had to trust in God and follow His commands. They included what and how to eat. What to harvest. However, it wasn't long when their chronic complaining about food began. They didn't trust in God's promise and leadership. Something called manna was provided for them daily. (No one is really sure what that was, what it tasted like or how it was made). The point is, God supplied their food and yet they complained. They wanted something else. They didn't trust in God. They wanted the foods of their desires, not the food God was providing them.

Similarly, Adam and Eve had all the food they needed as provided by God. Yet, when push came to shove, they wanted something else. Something more, something available and yet, unable to have whether it is by dictate or by distance. This food issue follows their history through the multiple dispersions.

Rejecting God

In the book of 1 Samuel, the prophet goes to God and laments how the people have rejected him as a leader.

God corrects Samuel and explains they did not reject him, Samuel. They rejected God who spoke through Samuel.

This reflection shows how God's way and direction is supplanted by one of human desire. God gives them a king with a very stern and sober warning as in 1Sam 8. It reflects the turning from God to the advice and ruler ship of one other than God. A form of idolatry, spiritual adultery, just as Eve and Adam did in the Garden.

Debt

The Bible repeatedly warns of debt, there are dozens of verses on this subject. The years of the Jubilees carry with them the elimination and removal of debt. How does that reflect Eden?

A family's child is their future. The child to be born in Eden represented all future, of mankind as well as the earth. Adam and Eve killed the future. They represented the past as well as their present. The future is built on these two building blocks. The past and present do not feed on the future which is what debt does. It robs the future for the benefit of the present. It kills the future. It kills our children's financial future as they are then left to pay off any remaining debt.

This is so pervasive and so easy for people to succumb to that the Adversary uses it to this day. In what could be called a cynical manipulation, the celebration of the birth of Yeshua, known as Christmas causes many to put themselves deep into debt for the sake of materialism. Whether or not it's the actual day is irrelevant at the moment and is a different discussion.

The point is, the celebration of the birth of the Son of God still carries with it to this day the feeding on the future. People are warned about spending too much during the Christmas season. They are warned to avoid going into debt for the sake of "presents". It's great to give but it's worse to go into debt just to be able to give someone some "thing", a toy, necktie, ornament for a shelf and so on. The reason for the day is overshadowed by the materialism of the day. The adversary overlaid the celebration of the birth of the Son of God with a subtle metaphor of the Original Sin, causing the sin to continue in another form. So, Eden is reflected once again.

War

War is a very similar reflection of Eden as debt. The future is killed off by the leaders, the parents as the young are sent off to fight and die in the course of battle. In the wilderness the children of Israel were commanded by God to go and defeat their enemies. When they did so under the direction and protection of God, none of their numbers died. The future was spared and preserved by

God. It was only when they went into battle of their own choice did, they suffer great numbers of dead and subsequent defeats.

Idolatry

Idolatry is pretty self-evident. It is the act of replacing God with another god of our own desire. In Eden Eve did this when she listened to the serpent and not God. Messiah reversed or defeated this when tempted in the wilderness. "You shall worship the Lord your God and Him only shall you serve!"

Murder

This has been covered with Cain. It is a continuation of Eden as we murder each other for personal vain reasons. It is a direct reflection of Eden as part of the inheritance of sin.

The New Covenant

These take on more intensity as they can be seen to directly reflect what took place in Eden. Any theologian who believes in the New Testament / New Covenant, will attest the reason Messiah came into this world was to remove sin which began in Eden and restore the connection to God.

The parallels are striking starting with the following.

The Temptations of Messiah

The temptations of Messiah also reflect what transpired in Eden.

The first temptation is that of food.

> *Now the serpent was more crafty than any beast of the field which the Lord God had*

made. And he said to the woman, "Indeed, has God said, 'You shall not eat from any tree of the garden'?" 2 The woman said to the serpent, "From the fruit of the trees of the garden we may eat; 3 but from the fruit of the tree which is in the middle of the garden, God has said, 'You shall not eat from it or touch it, or you will die.'" (Gen 3:1 NASB)

Messiah's temptation of food:

And the tempter came and said to Him, "If You are the Son of God, command that these stones become bread." 4 But He answered and said, "It is written, 'Man shall not live on bread alone, but on every word that proceeds out of the mouth of God.'" (Matthew 4:3 NASB)

And the devil said to Him, "If You are the Son of God, tell this stone to become bread." 4 And Jesus answered him, "It is written, 'Man shall not live on bread alone.'" (Luke 4: 3 NASB)

This is a rather obvious comparison. The temptation of food as was done in Eden as well as assuming the position of God. However, there are deeper significances when you start looking at the original words in the ancient language.

When digging deeper it can be seen the Adversary is not just tempting but taunting as well. He is being highly cynical and sarcastic. The Adversary isn't just mocking Yeshua as the "Bread of Life". He's making a direct reference to what took place in Eden. He is also mocking Him as the Son of God.

We look to Psalm 118 for a very interesting passage.

> *The stone which the builders rejected has become the chief corner stone. (Psalm 118: 22 NASB)*

The word in the original Hebrew is pronounced "evan", spelled אֶבֶן. We know this passage to be referencing Messiah, Yeshua. It references how He was rejected when He came. It can also be referencing His rejection as Immanuel when He came in Eden. More than this is what is encapsulated in the Hebrew word itself. It's basically comprised of two words, "Abba / Ave" for "Father" and "Ben" for "son". Combine them and have the word "evan" אֶבֶן.

This metaphor of Yeshua being the stone is what the Adversary is mocking in a most cynical way. He is commanding the Son of God to turn the stone to bread. This is what Eve and Adam did. They turned the Son of God, (son and father, the "evan") into "bread" for food. Satan was cynically and sarcastically praising his accomplishment in the Garden and mocking Yeshua at the same time.

The second Temptation is that of becoming Godlike.

The serpent said to the woman, "You surely will not die! 5 For God knows that in the day you eat from it your eyes will be opened, and you will be like God, knowing good and evil." (Gen 3:4 NASB)

Messiah is tempted to be like God the Father.

Then the devil *took Him into the holy city and had Him stand on the pinnacle of the temple, 6 and *said to Him, "If You are the Son of God, throw Yourself down; for it is written, 'He will command His angels concerning You'; and 'On their hands they will bear You up, So that You will not strike Your foot against a stone.'" (Matthew 4:5 NASB)

And he led Him to Jerusalem and had Him stand on the pinnacle of the temple, and said to Him, "If You are the Son of God, throw Yourself down from here; 10 for it is written, 'He will command His angels concerning You to guard You,' 11 and, 'On their hands they will bear You up, So that You will not strike Your foot against a stone.'" (Luke 4: 9 NASB)

Who, though existing in the form of God, did not consider being equal to God a thing to be grasped. (Philippians 2:6 TLV)

Messiah defeated this temptation with His humility.

Unlike Adam and Eve, He denied the temptation of being "God" or "godlike".

The third temptation was to follow someone other than God.

When the woman saw that the tree was good for food, and that it was a delight to the eyes, and that the tree was desirable to make one wise, she took from its fruit and ate; and she gave also to her husband with her, and he ate. 7 Then the eyes of both of them were opened, and they knew that they were naked; (Gen3:6 NASB)

Messiah is tempted to follow the Adversary instead of the Father.

Again, the devil *took Him to a very high mountain and *showed Him all the kingdoms of the world and their glory; 9 *and he said to Him, "All these things I will give You, if You fall down and worship me." (Matthew 4:8 NASB)*

And he led Him up and showed Him all the kingdoms of the world in a moment of time. 6 And the devil said to Him, "I will give You all this domain and its glory; for it has been handed over to me, and I give it to whomever I wish. 7 Therefore if You worship before me, it shall all be Yours." 8 Jesus answered him, "It is written, 'You shall worship the Lord your God and serve Him only.'" (Luke 4:5 NASB)

Instead of taking the vain promise of the ruler ship of the kingdoms, Yeshua rebuked the Adversary, thereby inheriting all of Creation itself as its King.

But answering, Yeshua told him, "It is written, 'You shall worship Adonai your God, and Him only shall you serve.'" (Luke 4:8 TLV)

And finally, He rebuffs the last of the temptations by throwing a somewhat cynical remark back at him. In that moment of victory Yeshua cast off the Adversary in a direct reprimand for demanding to be worshiped. It points to the very thing which the Adversary was attempting to do, replace God. He hated the fact he (the Adversary) is subservient to God and not the other way around.

Yeshua did not succumb to these temptations as we know. However, this is not about what He did so much as it is about what Eve and then Adam did. They gave into the same temptation for food. They gave into the same temptation to be godlike and they gave into the same temptation to listen to someone other than God.

In this process Yeshua one by one undid those particular actions committed in Eden. Later He pays the price for those actions, He takes on the punishment incurred by their disobedience.

Biblical Symbols

There are many symbols and metaphors used in the Bible. Many have already been mentioned such as fruit or trees.

Anyone who has seriously studied the Bible knows it speaks on a variety of levels and ways. It will have facts mixed with metaphors mixed with analogies, poetry, history, prophecy. Here are some of these metaphors which bear directly on the subject.

Pertinent to this thesis is the symbol or metaphor of the sacrificial lamb.

The Lamb

Take a moment to consider the symbolism of the lamb. The Messiah as the Lamb of God. The use of a lamb for the sin sacrifice.

A lamb is a baby sheep. It's is innocent and trusting. Why use the symbol of a baby sheep? Are older sheep somehow guilty of sin? Of course not. Only humans are capable of sin as we have the free will to disobey God. This particular symbol represents that which was slain at the time of Adam and Eve. It was a child, a baby, later to be symbolized by a lamb, a baby of another kind. We see in the sacrificial system how the animal is used to replace the human for the purposes of the covering of sin. It did not remove the sin, only temporarily covered it. This is similar to how God covered Adam and Eve with fur after they had sinned.

The Lamb was and is used to be a metaphor of the Son of God. I am suggesting this symbol was begun as a result of the actions of Adam and Eve as they in essence "sacrificed" the Son of God when He was still a child, a baby. So many tend to only think of Yeshua as a baby, lying there in the manger, watched over by caring parents.

It may be because it's a much happier vision than that of the

man hanging on the execution stake, cross or in essence

"tree". It is a pretty gruesome image.

More Parallels in the New Testament

In Jerusalem Yeshua was examined by the leaders and there was found no defect it was seen He was good and without blemish.

> *Then Pilate said to the chief priests and the crowds, "I find no guilt in this man." (Luke 23:4 NASB)*

> *having examined Him before you, I have found no guilt in this man regarding the charges which you make against Him. 15 No, nor has Herod, for he sent Him back to us; and behold, nothing deserving death has been done by Him. (Luke 23:14 NASB)*

In Eden Eve saw the fruit was a delight to her eyes and good for food.

> *So when the woman saw that the tree was good for food, that it was pleasant to the eyes, and a tree desirable to make one wise, (Gen 3:6 TLV)*

She basically "found no fault in it".

Next comes almost a total replay of Eden, only in reverse. Messiah and the disciples have the Passover Seder. They eat the "body and blood". The event called "The Last Supper" completely reflects what took place in Eden. However, this time there is an addition to the event which had been repeated for centuries. The Messiah Yeshua made the direct connection of Himself to the meal. This was the blatant connection of himself to what took place in Eden.

It all pointed to the reason Messiah came into this world in the first place. It was on account of what took place in Eden. He came to reconcile mankind back to God, because of Adam and Eve. The separation which began in Eden. Mankind was from Eden on, under the death penalty and subject to the bondage of death.

> *Therefore, since the children share in flesh and blood, He Himself likewise also*

partook of the same, that through death
He might render powerless him who had
the power of death, that is, the devil, 15
and might free those who through fear of
death were subject to slavery all their
lives. (Heb 2:14 NASB)

Messiah's last day and hours were an undoing of the events in Eden. Working its way backwards there was the meal where He tells them to eat His flesh and drink His blood. Later, the next morning He is killed, nailed to the execution stake or cross. Using just Matthew's account, we read:

As they were eating, He said, "Truly I say
to you that one of you will betray Me" (MT
26:21 NASB)

The Son of Man is to go, just as it is written
of Him; but woe to that man by whom the
Son of Man is betrayed (MT 26:24 NASB)

One of them did betray Him, both in Jerusalem and previously in Eden. In Jerusalem it was Judas Iscariot, in

Eden it was Eve and Adam. But it was in reverse order.

The body and blood were eaten, then the betrayal.

> *While they were eating, Yeshua took some bread, and after a blessing, He broke it and gave it to the disciples, and said, "Take, eat; this is My body." 27 And when He had taken a cup and given thanks, He gave it to them, saying, "Drink from it, all of you; 28 for this is My blood of the covenant, which is poured out for many for forgiveness of sins. (Mt26:26 NASB)*

One thing to add to the point of Yeshua using the bread to represent His body is the place of His birth. Many know how He was born in Bethlehem then later grew up in Nazareth. But not many in the Christian world know what the name "Bethlehem" means. It's comprised of two Hebrew words, "beth" or in the Hebrew "beit" (bay-eet) and lechem. Beth means "house" and lechem means "bread". The "bread of life" was born in the "house of bread" or in essence a bakery. There are no coincidences in the Bible! From His birth He was compared to food. This reinforces what the Adversary said when he tempted Yeshua with food.

Now look at the famous passage from the book of Luke.

> *Now Joseph also went up from the Galilee, out of the town of Natzeret to Judah, to the city of David, which is called Bethlehem, because he was from the house and family of David. 5 He went to register with Miriam, who was engaged to him and was pregnant. 6 But while they were there, the time came for her to give birth 7 and she gave birth to her firstborn son. She wrapped Him in strips of cloth and set Him down in a manger, (Luke 1: 4 TLV)*

Another interesting part of this which is directly on point is the phrase "set Him down in a manger". Many if not most assume that refers to the place where the birth took place, the cave or sukka, the dwelling they were in. This is incorrect. A manger was a container for animal feed such as cattle, horses, sheep and similar livestock. The original Greek word was "phatne". Both words describe a place where the food was placed for the animals to draw on.

A common interpretation points to the humility of His birth, being born poor and in a stable. The point here is, from His birth He was compared to food. That comparison was not initiated at the Last Supper. He was born in the house of bread (a bakery) and was set in a feeding trough. He is known as the Bread of Life. His existence is compared to food beginning in Genesis.

Another subtle aspect of this is the overall picture of His birthplace. His humble birth could be shown in a number of different ways, but in a place where animals were kept is interesting. With Adam and Eve in Eden, all that was present with them were the created animals. At

Yeshua's birth, all that was present with them were the animals.

Are these all merely more "coincidences"?

Cannibalism

Yeshua blatantly made the comparison of the food at the Last Supper (Passover Seder) to His body and its direct connection to the sin of mankind. It is common knowledge cannibalism is forbidden in the Bible. Yet, Messiah tells the disciples to in essence commit cannibalism! This confused the disciples at first. What they did not understand was this was all symbolic. Primarily of the sin in Eden. Eden was playing out once again.

Messiah Yeshua was then taken, scourged, being covered in His blood. He is lead to the place of execution and there He is nailed to the stake or cross. The final blow being a spear thrust into His side with blood and water gushing out.

All this happened in reverse to reverse what took place in Eden. As He hung there dying, he declares "it is finished". He was declaring sin had been removed. Which sin? That of Adam and Eve, the reason Messiah came.

He cries out "Father, forgive them, they don't know what they are doing!" This was not just for those who were behind His execution. Included in that prayer was the forgiveness of all of us and our sins as well. However, what is forgotten in all the drama and most is important is the reason He came and died in the first place. To undo what Adam and Eve had done. As the Scriptures state:

> *Therefore, just as through one man sin entered into the world, and death through sin, and so death spread to all men, because all sinned— 13 for until the Law sin was in the world, but sin is not imputed when there is no law. 14 Nevertheless death reigned from Adam until Moses, even over those who had not sinned in the likeness of the offense of Adam, who is a type of Him who was to come. 15 But the free gift is not like the transgression. For if by the transgression of the one the many*

died, much more did the grace of God and the gift by the grace of the one Man, Jesus Christ, abound to the many. 16 The gift is not like that which came through the one who sinned; for on the one hand the judgment arose from one transgression resulting in condemnation, but on the other hand the free gift arose from many transgressions resulting in justification. 17 For if by the transgression of the one, death reigned through the one, much more those who receive the abundance of grace and of the gift of righteousness will reign in life through the One, Jesus Christ. 18 So then as through one transgression there resulted condemnation to all men, even so through one act of righteousness there resulted justification of life to all men. 19 For as through the one man's disobedience the many were made sinners, even so through the obedience of the One the many will be made righteous. (Rom 5:12 NASB)

While dying Yeshua cried "my God, my God, why have your forsaken me?" quoting Psalm 22.

With both hands in the upward position, just as a child reaches up to his or her parents, he cried to them. He was in the process also reflecting what took place in Eden, asking why they had forsaken him (the child in Eden). All of these events were a repeat and reflection of Eden where sin entered the world and mankind lost the connection to God. Only this time sin was being removed from the world, the actions of Adam and Eve were being replayed and reversed.

After Yeshua was crucified, he was dead for three days until the day of First Fruits as described in the book of Leviticus. On that day He rose from the dead. Notice the term for the Messiah, "**First Fruits**" of the Resurrection; **Yeshua is the first fruits**. The metaphor is not only pointing to the Messiah who would and did come but also to His original arrival and subsequent premature death.

Messiah was risen from the dead and able to dwell as God with man as was originally intended by God. Every year the nations and peoples of the earth are commanded to come to Jerusalem to be with Messiah and celebrate the time Sukkoth or "Tabernacles" which simply means to dwell. God wants to dwell with us, we His people and He our God.

The Two Loaves

In Leviticus the Lord explains the appointed days, the "moedim". At the end of the period of unleavened bread is the day of "First Fruits". The details of the day begin on Leviticus 23:16.

> *You shall count fifty days to the day after the seventh sabbath; then you shall present a new grain offering to the Lord. (Lev 23:16 NASB)*

The fifty days is where we get the term "Pentecost," "pente" being fifty.

Beginning in verse 17 the details of the two loaves begins.

> *You shall bring in from your dwelling places two loaves of bread for a wave offering, made of two-tenths of an ephah; they shall be of a fine flour, baked with leaven as first fruits to the Lord. 18 Along*

*with the bread you shall present seven
one-year old male lambs without defect,
and a bull of the herd and two rams; they
are to be a burnt offering to the Lord, with
their grain offering and their drink
offerings, an offering by fire of a soothing
aroma to the Lord. 19 You shall also offer
one male goat for a sin offering and two
male lambs one year old for a sacrifice of
peace offerings. 20 The priest shall then
wave them with the bread of the first fruits
for a wave offering with two lambs before
the Lord; they are to be holy to the Lord
for the priest. (Lev 23:17 NASB)*

On that day, the High Priest is to wave two fresh

loaves as a "wave offering". These along with two lambs

are presented as an offering and sacrifice.

*The priest shall then wave them with the
bread of the first fruits for a wave offering
with two lambs before the Lord; they are
to be holy to the Lord for the priest. (Lev
23:20 NASB)*

The question is, why two loaves? What is the

significance of two loaves in particular? There are many

theories on the reason for two loaves. There is no clear and definitive reason for why two.

Some say they represent the need for two witnesses as is required for authenticating a crime, divorce, or with the two witnesses prophesied to come in the end times.

It could be, they represent the divided kingdom, Israel and Judah. They may represent the two trees in Eden.

Some have likened the two loaves to represent the Jews and Gentiles in the One New Man concept which is spoken of in the Scriptures.

These all may be true, each in their own context and way. However, there may be even more to the meaning of there being two loaves on the day of First Fruits.

First Fruits is the day commonly referred to as Pentecost. It is the day it is said Moses came down with the Torah and discovered the sin taking place among the Israelites. It is also more commonly understood to be the day the Holy Spirit descended on the Apostles in Jerusalem.

What happens is, on this when the power of the Holy Spirit, the other parent of the Son of God is displayed, two loaves of bread along with a lamb for each are offered. Two loaves of bread along with two babies (represented in metaphor) are presented. Two analogies of food accompanied by a baby are shown on the day of **First Fruits**. In the name of the day as declared by God in the book of Leviticus is the key, the **First FRUITS**. The First Fruit of Creation and the First Fruit of the Resurrection. Therein lies the deeper mystery of the two loaves.

A major aspect of this is two loaves do not stand alone, they are coupled with two lambs as stated in Lev 23:20. All the other commentaries may be true, but in the context of First FRUITS, these can also be seen as the two births. With the basis of this thesis in mind, the connection is clear, the loaves and lambs represent the two births. The first in Eden and the second in Bethlehem. The two births have something in common as described, they also represent to very interesting meals.

The day of First Fruits is the culmination of all that happened from Eden through to and including the Resurrection. Death has been defeated. The loaves and the lambs are the analogies of the two meals which took place. The first meal causing the fall and the second meal reversing it. This is the underlying reason for there being two loaves along with two baby lambs.

Later this symbolism could include most if not all of the theories many theologians have speculated. Not the least of which representing the two prophets of the End Times, the two parts of the Bible, the two halves of the One New Man, Jew and Gentile and the other similar metaphors of two.

Born Again

Another aspect of the two loaves and the two births is the pattern of being "Born Again." As Messiah stated to Nicodemus, "That which is born of the flesh is flesh, that which is born of the spirit is spirit". Could what took place in Eden, then followed by what took place in Bethlehem be a shadow of the Born Again motif? The pattern beginning in Eden, being born, then being Born Again in Bethlehem?

The first birth is the one I am alleging happened in Eden. But as death entered the world with the death of that child, creation itself became subject to death. It all must be reborn of the Spirit. It must be "born again." This we see happen in Bethlehem when the Spirit comes upon Miriam and she gives birth to the One who will save the earth and creation from the death which resulted from the actions in

Eden. It is He, Messiah who holds the power of Creation and upholds it, binding it all together. By the Adversary attacking the child in Eden, he put all of the new creation in jeopardy. God as we know had a plan for redemption and salvation.

The model of being born again begins in Eden. This is where this template or pattern is set forth. The Child of God, the Son of God would need to be born again to dwell with man the way God intended.

This may seem confusing but, what needs to be done is to separate the two births from each other. They do not occur within the same context. What separates them is the concept of sin. The first birth was in a sinless world. The need for the second, for a Messiah, a Savior, our Yeshua, our salvation, that need did not come about until after the fall. The entire Bible, all of Scripture is an answer to Genesis 1 through 3. From Genesis 4 and on, it's all about the new birth to come the redemption, reclamation of man and creation, back to God.

The bulk of the Scriptures are detailing His coming to redeem mankind and restore us all to the condition found in Genesis 1 through 3. Many believers and scholars wonder why there is a second creation depicted in Genesis 2, what are called the "Generations of Adam". This second creation again is a shadow of the two births, the two creations.

Sin is atoned for

In a letter to the Jewish believers in Jerusalem the following statements are made. Once again, the connection to Eden can be seen in the background. Sin began in Eden, sin ended at the death of Messiah.

Messiah's Death Fulfills God's Will

Therefore, when He comes into the world, He says, "Sacrifice and offering You have not desired, but a body You have prepared for Me; 6 In whole burnt offerings and sacrifices for sin You have taken no pleasure. 7 "Then I said, 'Behold, I have come (In the scroll of the book it is written of Me) To do Your will, O God.'" 8 After saying above, "Sacrifices and offerings and whole burnt offerings and sacrifices for sin You have not desired, nor have You taken pleasure in them" (which are offered according to the Law), 9 then He said, "Behold, I have come to do Your will." He takes away the first in order to establish the second. 10 By this will we have been sanctified through the offering of the body of Jesus Christ once for all. (Hebrews 10:5 NASB)

It is through Messiah's death we are sanctified.

Every priest stands daily ministering and offering time after time the same sacrifices, which can never take away sins; 12 but He, having offered one sacrifice for sins for all time, sat down at the right hand of God, 13 waiting from that time onward until His enemies be made a footstool for His feet. 14 For by one offering He has perfected for all time those who are sanctified. 15 And the Holy Spirit also testifies to us; for after saying, 16 "This is the covenant that I will make with them after those days, says the Lord: I will put My laws upon their heart, and on their mind I will write them," He then says, 17 "And their sins and their lawless deeds I will remember no more." 18 Now where there is forgiveness of these things, there is no longer any offering for sin. (Hebrews 10:11 NASB)

Sin has been removed. Not from the earth or human history but from our inherited punishment as a result of what took place in Eden. Our own spiritual "karma" derived from Adam is removed, atoned for by the death of the one who the sin was perpetrated against in the first place.

The incident in Eden is depicted throughout the entirety of the Bible. From Genesis and the undefined sin through Revelation and the Lamb that was slain at the creation of the world. Only one possible action can answer all of these questions, aspects and elements. There could be only one reason Messiah had to do what He did to remove this human curse. All the elements of the Scriptures bear witness to that one particular event in Eden.

We are now a new creature, set free from the bondage to the sin committed in Eden. The penalty has been paid as depicted in the Scriptures.

How will we use our freedom? To continue to sin or to put the evil behind us and move on, a new creature under Heaven. It is up to each of us on our own.

Pattern of the Brothers

Another pattern which keeps recurring regards the relationship between the older and younger brothers. Most importantly that as it relates to inheritance. In those times the inheritance would include any monetary wealth, flocks and herds, but more importantly land. This pattern shows up over and over again. The first time it appears with significance is with Ishmael and Isaac. Ishmael and his mother are cast out after the birth of Isaac.

Later, Isaac's wife Rebecca has the two sons who are battling in the womb, Esau and Jacob.

> *But the children struggled together within her; and she said, "If it is so, why then am I this way?" (Gen 25:22 NASB)*

Esau is the oldest, the first born and thereby would be the one who is first in line for inheritance.

So she went to inquire of the Lord. 23 The Lord said to her,

"Two nations are in your womb;

And two peoples will be separated from your body;

And one people shall be stronger than the other;

And the older shall serve the younger."

24 When her days to be delivered were fulfilled, behold, there were twins in her womb. 25 Now the first came forth red, all over like a hairy garment; and they named him Esau. 26 Afterward his brother came forth with his hand holding on to Esau's heel, so his name was called Jacob;... (Gen 25:22 NASB)

Jacob and his mother Rebecca trick Isaac into blessing Jacob with the inheritance due the first born. Esau also trades his inheritance before that for a meal, colored blood red.

When Jacob had cooked stew, Esau came in from the field and he was famished; 30

*and Esau said to Jacob, "Please let me
have a swallow of that red stuff there, for
I am famished." Therefore his name was
called Edom. 31 But Jacob said, "First
sell me your birthright." 32 Esau said,
"Behold, I am about to die; so of what use
then is the birthright to me?" 33 And
Jacob said, "First swear to me"; so he
swore to him, and sold his birthright to
Jacob. 34 Then Jacob gave Esau bread
and lentil stew; and he ate and drank, and
rose and went on his way. Thus Esau
despised his birthright. (Gen 25:29 NASB)*

This is a very simplified explanation of the pattern

being presented. There is also a direct link between

Ishmael and Esau as Esau marries one of the daughters of

Ishmael.

*Now these are the records of the
generations of Esau (that is, Edom). 2
Esau took his wives from the daughters of
Canaan: Adah the daughter of Elon the
Hittite, and Oholibamah the daughter of
Anah and the granddaughter of Zibeon the
Hivite; 3 also Basemath, Ishmael's*

daughter, the sister of Nebaioth. (Gen 36:1 NASB)

The point here is the older brothers are passed over for the younger. Whether it is being cast away and disinherited or through selling off one's birth right for food. The older is replaced by the younger. This shows up again with Tamar and the twins.

It came about at the time she was giving birth, that behold, there were twins in her womb. 28 Moreover, it took place while she was giving birth, one put out a hand, and the midwife took and tied a scarlet thread on his hand, saying, "This one came out first." 29 But it came about as he drew back his hand, that behold, his brother came out. Then she said, "What a breach you have made for yourself!" So he was named Perez. 30 Afterward his brother came out who had the scarlet thread on his hand; and he was named Zerah. (Genesis 38: 27 NASB)

The older here is marked with a scarlet thread. As discussed earlier, the word for scarlet contains a variant of the word for blood. The older is marked with blood red.

Then the younger comes out. It is this younger who takes

somehow becomes the first "born" who is an ancestor of

Messiah Yeshua. The younger becomes the inheritor. In

this case his descendant Yeshua inherits all of Creation.

Now consider the parable of the prodigal son.

> *And He said, "A man had two sons. 12 The*
> *younger of them said to his father,*
> *'Father, give me the share of the estate*
> *that falls to me.' So he divided his wealth*
> *between them. 13 And not many days*
> *later, the younger son gathered everything*
> *together and went on a journey into a*
> *distant country, and there he squandered*
> *his estate with loose living. 14 Now when*
> *he had spent everything, a severe famine*
> *occurred in that country, and he began to*
> *be impoverished. 15 So he went and hired*
> *himself out to one of the citizens of that*
> *country, and he sent him into his fields to*
> *feed swine. 16 And he would have gladly*
> *filled his stomach with the pods that the*
> *swine were eating, and no one was giving*

anything to him. 17 But when he came to his senses, he said, 'How many of my father's hired men have more than enough bread, but I am dying here with hunger! 18 I will get up and go to my father, and will say to him, "Father, I have sinned against heaven, and in your sight; 19 I am no longer worthy to be called your son; make me as one of your hired men." ' 20 So he got up and came to his father. But while he was still a long way off, his father saw him and felt compassion for him, and ran and embraced him and kissed him. 21 And the son said to him, 'Father, I have sinned against heaven and in your sight; I am no longer worthy to be called your son.' 22 But the father said to his slaves, 'Quickly bring out the best robe and put it on him, and put a ring on his hand and sandals on his feet; 23 and bring the fattened calf, kill it, and let us eat and celebrate; 24 for this son of mine was dead and has come to life again; he was lost and has been found.' And they began to celebrate.

25 "Now his older son was in the field, and when he came and approached the house, he heard music and dancing. 26

And he summoned one of the servants and begin inquiring what these things could be. 27 And he said to him, 'Your brother has come, and your father has killed the fattened calf because he has received him back safe and sound.' 28 But he became angry and was not willing to go in; and his father came out and began pleading with him. 29 But he answered and said to his father, 'Look! For so many years I have been serving you and I have never neglected a command of yours; and yet you have never given me a young goat, so that I might celebrate with my friends; 30 but when this son of yours came, who has devoured your wealth with prostitutes, you killed the fattened calf for him.' 31 And he said to him, 'Son, you have always been with me, and all that is mine is yours. 32 But we had to celebrate and rejoice, for this brother of yours was dead and has begun to live, and was lost and has been found.'" (Luke 15:11 NASB)

This is not about Yeshua as the older brother specifically. It is what it is, a parable. But the parallels are there. If Messiah, Yeshua, the First Born at Creation is the older brother, we, the believers are the younger brother(s); and sisters of course. We are the ones who went astray squandering our lives away.

Just as the parable describes, the Father turns to the son and states: "you are always with me, everything I have is yours". This is completely true of the relationship of God the Father and the Messiah, His Son. The parable is about returning to faith, returning to a relationship of parent to the child as we, through belief in Messiah regain that connection to God. Thus God the Father and the Son, Messiah Yeshua rejoice as the lost sheep one by one return to Him.

What's in a Name?

In the Scriptures we see where Joseph is spoken to about the upcoming birth of Messiah through his betrothed Miriam.

> *But when he had considered this, behold, an angel of the Lord appeared to him in a dream, saying, "Joseph, son of David, do not be afraid to take Mary as your wife; for the Child who has been conceived in her is of the Holy Spirit. 21 She will bear a Son; and you shall call His name Jesus, for He will save His people from their sins." (Matthew 1:20 NASB)*

However, an important point is made regarding this in the verse immediately following it. It speaks of the prophecy from Isaiah.

> *Now all this took place to fulfill what was spoken by the Lord through the prophet: 23 "Behold, the virgin shall be with child and shall bear a Son, and they shall call*

His name Immanuel," which translated means, "God with us." (Matthew 1:22 NASB)

Therefore the Lord Himself will give you a sign: Behold, a virgin will be with child and bear a son, and she will call His name Immanuel. (Isaiah 7:14 NASB)

So why the two names?

One very simple and logical reason is the name Immanuel is merely a descriptive name, kind of like a nick name. However, the name Immanuel would aptly befit the First Born in Eden as that is precisely who and what He was at that moment. He was not as yet in the role of the Salvation or in the Hebrew "Yeshua". God throughout the Scriptures is known as the God with no name. It isn't until God is speaking to Moses, He refers to His name in the four Hebrew letters yud heh vav heh, what many today pronounce as "Jehovah" which is inherently incorrect. There are too many opinions on how to properly pronounce the four letters as well as what they and the Name itself actually mean. That controversy is for another time. The point being, the First Born was never given a Name officially, though He would have been Immanuel, God with us. Since the Biblical names tend to have specific meanings, as presented earlier, this prophecy could be not only alluding to the coming Messiah but to the First Born whose Name could and should have been Immanuel.

Here is a great example of how names in the Bible carry very specific meanings. Consider what is hidden in Genesis 5 with the names of the generations following Adam

These are the meanings of the names as words.

Adam =   Man
Seth =   Appointed
Enosh =   Mortal

Cainan = Sorrow

Mahalalel = The Blessed God

Jared = Shall Come Down

Enoch = Teaching

Methuselah = His death shall bring

Lamech = (the) Despairing

Noah = Comfort (rest).

"Man is appointed mortal sorrow; the Blessed God shall come down teaching that His death shall bring to the despairing, comfort."

The Tree of Life

Also, in the midst of the garden the other mysterious tree, the Tree of Life. This discussion would not be complete without mentioning this other "tree".

The tree of life "Etz ha Chai-eem", עֵץ הַחַיִּים first appears in Genesis 2. It is described as being "in the midst of the Garden" along with the tree of the knowledge of good and evil

After Adam and Eve have sinned and are fallen from grace, God says: "lest he put forth his hand, and take also of the tree of life, and eat, and live forever" God banishes Adam and Eve from Eden.

Angels, namely "cherubim" were then placed at the east end of the Garden to guard the way to the Tree of Life. This in order to prevent their returning to the Garden. The

Tree of Life has become the subject of some debate as to whether or not the tree of the knowledge of good and evil is the same tree.

The symbolism of a tree and its potential meaning is open to a vastly wide variety of interpretations. Some liken it to the Cross, others to a quest for eternal life.

The symbolism of a tree as a "tree of life" across a multitude of cultures is almost universally seen as representing eternal life in some way. A picture of a connection to the earth where its roots are burrowed deep. Then reaching up to the heavens with its branches, ever growing closer to the Divine. It can represent a family as in a human family. It can represent a gradual growth of something. It can symbolize serenity or a source of food, a place of rest under its shady branches or of safety in its branches by the creatures who nest there.

As with the word "fruit" which has been shown to mean far more than just a piece of vegetation, the symbolism for the word "tree" is just as misleading if one only reads superficially or hyper-literally.

Augustine of Hippo in his writing "The City of God" wrote of the Tree of Life but did not define its meaning or symbolism and left it open to a person's own interpretation. John Calvin, Karl Budde, Thomas Aquinas all had their own opinions on what this tree was and represented.

Even Judaism has its own theory which tends to have a more mythological answer. The tree of life in Eden supposedly represents a "tree of souls" where new souls are produced, they then go into the "Guf" or the Treasury of Souls. The Angel Gabriel would reach into the Guf and take out the first soul in his hand and hand it to the Angel of Conception Lailah. It all sounds like a way to answer a question they had not yet figured out.

The phrase "Tree of Life" appears a number of times throughout the Scriptures other than just in Genesis. These when looked at closely begin to put the pieces together.

The first tree is one of knowledge of good and evil, this is representative of the Holy Spirit. The second tree is the Tree of Life. This represents Messiah. Both were present as the book of Genesis describes. The spirit of God hovering over the waters along with the Word of God who spoke everything into being.

The first tree was knowledge whereas the second is that of wisdom. When Messiah said He came to fulfill the Torah, the words used more precisely mean to bring proper understanding. He was teaching the correct understanding and interpretation of the Torah. It is a Rabbinic teaching that when Messiah comes, He will bring proper understanding of Torah. This is exactly what Yeshua was saying He was there for and doing.

So, what is proper understanding? It is basically wisdom. Wisdom is more akin to understanding whereas knowledge is primarily information based. Wisdom brings understanding of that information. Wisdom without knowledge is weak, knowledge without wisdom is confusion. The following shows how wisdom is related to the second tree.

> *"So now, children, listen to me! Blessed are those who keep my ways. 33 Heed discipline and be wise, and do not neglect it. 34 Blessed is the one who listens to me, watching daily at my gates, waiting at my doorposts. 35 For whoever finds me finds life and obtains favor from Adonai. (Proverbs 8:32 TLV emphasis mine)*

Solomon is saying the understanding of God's instructions, teachings and commands are the way to eternal life. This would then equate to the Tree of Life. The Word of God is the Tree of Life. Yeshua is the Word of God and therefore the Tree of Life, the only path to eternal life.

The fruit of the righteous is a tree of life, and he who is wise wins souls. (Proverbs 11: 30 NASB)

How blessed is the man who finds wisdom and the man who gains understanding. 14 For her profit is better than the profit of silver and her gain better than fine gold. 15 She is more precious than jewels; and nothing you desire compares with her. 16 Long life is in her right hand; In her left hand are riches and honor. 17 Her ways are pleasant ways and all her paths are peace. 18 She is a tree of life to those who take hold of her, and happy are all who hold her fast. 19 The Lord by wisdom founded the earth, by understanding He

*established the heavens. (Proverbs 3:13
NASB)*

We can see here how it mirrors the description of creation in Genesis. Wisdom is a path of peace, pleasantness. Yeshua stated He is the way or path. It says, "the Lord by wisdom founded the earth". We read the following in the Gospel of John.

In the beginning was the Word, and the Word was with God, and the Word was God. 2 He was in the beginning with God. 3 All things came into being through Him, and apart from Him nothing came into being that has come into being. 4 In Him was life, and the life was the Light of men. (John 1:1 NASB)

Proverbs accurately connects wisdom with the Word of God (Messiah Yeshua) and thereby with the Tree of Life. Whereas the Tree of Knowledge of Good and Evil, basically a tree of knowledge is very subtly different as it is what moves the waters.

Solomon then states:

By His knowledge the deeps were broken up and the skies drip with dew. (Proverbs 3:20 NASB)

In Genesis we read:

and the Spirit of God was moving over the surface of the waters. (Gen 1:2 NASB)

The Spirit of God was hovering over the face of the waters, a couple of passages later we read what happens with those waters.

And God said, Let there be a firmament in the midst of the waters, and let it divide the waters from the waters. 7 And God made the firmament, and divided the waters which were under the firmament from the waters which were above the firmament: and it was so. (Gen 1:6 NASB)

Again, Solomon accurately depicts the two trees and their relationship to the Holy Spirit and the Messiah. The "Tree of the Knowledge of Good and Evil" is the first tree representing the Holy Spirit. The Tree of Life is that

of wisdom and is thus the Messiah. These are the only two

aspects of God which have any direct contact and

interrelationship with man, and both were present in Eden

interacting with Adam and Eve. Remember what is said in

the letter of 1Timothy.

> *the blessed and only Ruler, the King of kings and the Lord of lords, 16 who alone has immortality, dwelling in unapproachable light, whom no man has seen or is able to see. (1Tim 6: 15 TLV)*

The Father in His Heaven is unapproachable. It is

said even the angles have to hide their eyes in His presence.

> *In the year of King Uzziah's death, I saw Adonai sitting on a throne, high and lifted up, and the train of His robe filled the Temple. 2 Seraphim were standing above Him. Each had six wings: <u>with two he covered his face</u> and with two he covered his feet, and with two he flew. (Isaiah 6:1 TLV)*

Isaiah was not in Heaven but was shown a vision of Heaven.

Returning to the point being made about the Tree of Knowledge representing the Son of God, here is a metaphor Yeshua used to help underscore this point.

> "I am the true vine, and My Father is the vinedresser. 2 Every branch in Me that does not bear fruit, He takes away; and every branch that bears fruit, He prunes it so that it may bear more fruit. 3 You are already clean because of the word which I have spoken to you. 4 Abide in Me, and I in you. As the branch cannot bear fruit of itself unless it abides in the vine, so neither can you unless you abide in Me. (John 15:1 NASB)

Now consider the very well-known passage of John 3.

> As Moses lifted up the serpent in the wilderness, even so must the Son of Man be lifted up; 15 so that whoever believes

will in Him have eternal life. 16 "For God so loved the world, that He gave His only begotten Son, that whoever believes in Him shall not perish, but have eternal life. 17 For God did not send the Son into the world to judge the world, but that the world might be saved through Him. (John 3:14 NASB)

He who believes in the Son has eternal life; but he who does not obey the Son will not see life, but the wrath of God abides on him." (John 3:36 NASB)

This compares and contrasts directly with how Adam and Eve were prevented from receiving of the Tree of Life.

Now this is eternal life: that they know you, the only true God, and Yeshua the Messiah whom you have sent. (John 17:3 TLV)

and I give eternal life to them, and they will never perish; and no one will snatch them out of My hand. 29 My Father, who has given them to Me, is greater than all; and no one is able to snatch them out of the Father's hand. 30 I and the Father are one." (John 10:28-30 NASB)

For the wages of sin is death, but the gift of God is eternal life in Messiah Yeshua our Lord. (Romans 6:23 NASB)

So that, just as sin reigned in death, so also grace might reign through righteousness to bring <u>eternal life through Messiah Yeshua our Lord.</u> (Romans 5:21 NASB)

I write these things to you who <u>believe in the name of the Son of God</u> so that you may know <u>that you have eternal life.</u> (1 John 5:13 NASB)

It is shown again and again the relationship of Yeshua the Messiah as the bringer of eternal life just as stated in Genesis the Tree of Life is the holder of eternal life.

However, another paradox comes when trying to place the Fruit of the first tree along with that of the second tree, the Tree of Life. Then waking up in the middle of the night the words of Yeshua came to me.

> *"I am the Alpha and the Omega," says the Lord God, "who is, and who was, and who is to come, the Almighty." (Revelation 1:8 NASB)*

> *I am the Alpha and the Omega, the Beginning and the End, the First and the Last." (Rev 22:13 NASB)*

He is the beginning and the end. He is at the beginning and at the end. We can easily read where He is present at the end, but where is He at the beginning? True He is there as the Creator in the form of the Word of God speaking things into being. As he says, "the Almighty". Could this not also relate to His being there at the beginning when sin entered the world and then again at the end of it? He is therefore both the victim and resolution of Eden, all reenacted at the appointed time in Jerusalem.

God had both in place, knowing the end from the

beginning.

He who was and is and is to come.

The Bronze Serpent

Then the Lord said to Moses, "Make a fiery serpent, and set it on a standard; and it shall come about, that everyone who is bitten, when he looks at it, he will live." 9 And Moses made a bronze serpent and set it on the standard; and it came about, that if a serpent bit any man, when he looked to the bronze serpent, he lived. (Numbers 21:8 NASB)

Hebrew for the word serpent is the same as in

Genesis "nachash" נָחָשׁ

The symbol used to protect the Israelites was coincidentally a serpent, a symbol of the sin which began in Eden. Using this as a symbol of forgiveness and protection from sin appears to create a contradiction. However, when examined a bit closer it actually fits very well. The Israelites who just left Egypt after spending four hundred years there would have understood its meaning to that culture.

This particular image of the serpent symbolized the mythos of the protection of the Egyptian female deity Renenutet with her deific son Nepri and the spirit or "Ka" in the afterlife.

The Uraeus Cobra is mainly seen as the typical cobra ready to strike; raised up and its hood open. The term "uraeus" is a Greek word and is believed to be derived from the Egyptian words for "She who rears up". The cobra depicted is the particular species known as the "Naja haje". The Uraeus symbolized a variety of things from upper and lower Egypt whether to the sun or the king and a variety of deities. The meanings in particular which are on point to this discussion are the only ones being mentioned. The others can be attributed to the convolution of the Egyptian religion of the time.

The ancient Israelites had just come from Egypt with its multiple gods and pagan practices with their many signs and symbols. They understood the symbol of the protective snake and what it meant, Renenutet's protection. This understanding they had at that time has long been lost to the modern mindset. A good deal of their work load was to make bricks for the various building projects. Wealthy Egyptians would have their own tombs made of bricks; the symbols relating to death, souls and the afterlife were common knowledge to the Israelites who had just left Egypt. Just as people today have various funeral ceremonies and traditions which apply to all who die regardless of stature, so too the non-royals would want the same protection in the afterlife.

The Ureaus was the symbol of the protection of the spirit in the afterlife; an ancient ideology that the Semitics having just left Egypt still recognized and understood though may not have personally or collectively believed in. Interestingly, the Uraeus Cobra in funerary depictions was often shown as spitting fire. This fits perfectly with the term "fiery serpent" as the Bible describes them.

This underscores the direct association the cobra symbol had with death and the protection in the afterlife. (*So, the Lord sent fiery serpents among the people.*) They knew what the fire spitting serpents represented, not just death but a relationship to spiritual death as well.

This then has a direct correlation to the New Testament and Yeshua. These symbols were form of worship the Israelites were aware of at the time, they had come to at least generally understand them and had melded some into their own belief structure to varying degrees.

> *The people spoke against God and Moses,*
> *"Why have you brought us up out of Egypt*
> *to die in the wilderness? For there is no*
> *food and no water, and we loathe this*

miserable food." 6 The Lord sent fiery serpents among the people and they bit the people, so that many people of Israel died. 7 So the people came to Moses and said, "We have sinned, because we have spoken against the Lord and you; intercede with the Lord, that He may remove the serpents from us." And Moses interceded for the people. 8 Then the Lord said to Moses, "Make a fiery serpent, and set it on a standard; and it shall come about, that everyone who is bitten, when he looks at it, he will live." 9 And Moses made a bronze serpent and set it on the standard; and it came about, that if a serpent bit any man, when he looked to the bronze serpent, he lived. (Numbers 21:5 NASB)

As Moses lifted up the serpent in the wilderness, even so must the Son of Man be lifted up; 15 so that whoever believes will in Him have eternal life. (John 3:14 NASB)

So why would God have Moses raise up a serpent as a symbol of protection when in Genesis and Revelation, it is written how the serpent is ostensibly the "Satan". Plus, the serpents are the ones who are tormenting the Israelites at that time? Why use the raised symbol of a serpent as a sign of protection from the very same serpents biting and killing the Israelites?

Moses raised the symbol of the afterlife protection for the Israelites to come to; just as we are to come to the Cross of Messiah.

If the first sin committed in Eden is the murder of the First Born of Creation, He then not only represents the actual beginning of sin but is at the same time the protection and removal of that sin. Then in the wilderness the serpent, the symbol of the sin in Eden becomes the symbol of the protection and removal of the sin occurring at that time. This would mirror the two trees in Eden, the one from which sin began and the one which later ended sin and gave eternal life. Messiah is our protection from Death.

The mythology of Re the Sun God, says Isis created the "Uraeus" from spittle from the Sun God (probably due to the burning sensation from the spitted poison) mixed with the dust of the earth. Notice in the book of John the actions taken by Yeshua as he heals a blind man.

> When He had said this, He spat on the ground, and made clay of the spittle, and applied the clay to his eyes, 7 and said to him, "Go, wash in the pool of Siloam" (which is translated, Sent). So he went away and washed, and came back seeing. (John 9:6-7 NASB)

Do not confuse the similarities with an idea this story was gleaned from Egyptian mythology. Quite the contrary. Just as all of the plagues which befell Egypt was a polemic or rebuke of an Egyptian deity, so too this has behind it a rebuke of that pagan mythology.

Yeshua Himself made the direct correlation between Himself and that symbol in word, actions and symbolisms. He was not claiming to be any of the Egyptian deities or related to them or their worship. This just was another polemic against those, proving who the real God is, the God of Abraham, Isaac and Jacob, the God of Israel.

As shown, the New Testament states Messiah would be lifted up as the serpent Moses lifted up in the wilderness. The very same symbol Moses used in the wilderness to protect the Israelites from death was the symbol of sin and death.

This symbol and what it represented, was another step in the pattern or type for the coming of Yeshua who would be lifted up the same way and displayed for all to see and come to for the true and complete removal of sin and the protection from death. This is why the snake was used as the symbol of their protection from the snakes which were killing them. It symbolized sin and death and at the same time the protection from death and removal of the sin.

The bronze serpent which Moses had made lasted until the reign of Hezekiah son of Ahaz. The Israelites maintained it with a form of cultic idolatry which developed into a veneration of the raised serpent until it was destroyed by King Hezekiah.

> *He removed the high places and broke down the sacred pillars and cut down the Asherah. He also broke in pieces the bronze serpent that Moses had made, for until those days the sons of Israel burned incense to it; and it was called Nehushtan. (2Kings 18:4 NASB)*

In the Hebrew, the word transliterated as "Nehustan" is spelled נְחֻשְׁתָּן and comes from the root word "nachash", serpent.

To the culture of the early church in the Roman Empire, the cross was symbolic of death, a brutal, painful, public, suffering death.

To the Israelites during the time of the Exodus, the striking cobra was just as symbolic of suffering a painful death. With the Israelites the serpent was in particular a fiery serpent. In both cases the symbol of death became the symbol of salvation from death. One could see this as neutralizing death as well as the fear of death through its most significant representation.

It is interesting to note how the modern Christian faiths have adopted the symbol of the Cross and venerated it to a degree where it has become worshipped instead of the one who was hung on it. Venerated and worshipped just as the ancient Israelites did with the bronze snake symbol Moses raised in the wilderness. Thus, as the Bible states in 2Kings18 with Hezekiah King of Judah, the sacred pillars, wooden image and the bronze image were

destroyed. This is in obedience to God's command in

Deuteronomy 12:

> *You shall utterly destroy all the places*
> *where the nations whom you shall*
> *dispossess serve their gods, on the high*
> *mountains and on the hills and under*
> *every green tree. 3 You shall tear down*
> *their altars and smash their sacred pillars*
> *and burn their Asherim with fire, and you*
> *shall cut down the engraved images of*
> *their gods and obliterate their name from*
> *that place. 4 You shall not act like this*
> *toward the Lord your God. (Deut 12:2*
> *NASB)*

At the same time the sin is present, so too the way
out of it is also present.

> *Now the Torah came in so that*
> *transgression might increase. But where*
> *sin increased, grace overflowed even*
> *more. 21 so that just as sin reigned in*
> *death, so also grace might reign through*
> *righteousness, to eternal life through*
> *Messiah Yeshua our Lord. (Romans 5:20*
> *TLV)*

At the same time, the object of the sin was present in Eden, the removal of that sin was present. The object which caused death was present with that which allowed eternal life. The object which became their sin, was present with the object which would have removed sin's punishment. He then becomes sin, just as He was the source of their sin in Eden.

He made Him who knew no sin to be sin on our behalf, (2 Corinth 5:21 NASB)

So how does this all play out?

God through the Son (the Word) speaks all of creation into being. This so He (God) can dwell with the creature He specifically made to dwell with, man (and woman "mankind).

God is then in the Garden with Adam and the woman (later to be called Eve).

The Holy Spirit, "hovering over the waters", which can also depict the womb of a woman speaks the Light into the world. Eve conceives a child. "And that light is the light of men"

Eve, not knowing what is happening other than observance of other creatures around, then gives birth with a painless or minimally painful birthing. This is the First Born of Creation.

The Adversary disguised as a serpent, acting as just another of the beasts of the field, tricks Eve. He beguiles her with what serpents do and were doing at the time. They were eating theirs and others' defenseless young and newborns. Eve saw this concept and within her naiveté passed the suggestion on to Adam who acquiesced to her request. They murdered the child, piercing it before it was able to speak. The body of the child gushed out blood, splashing and covering their unclothed bodies with said blood. Being blood covered then becomes the look of being covered in sin.

It was at that point they knew they had done something terribly wrong. It was something they could not hide, even with leaves sewn together. Just as one weeps for an only child, the two felt the inherent guilt and hid themselves. They also at that moment realized they were no longer protected from God; they and their sin were naked before him. They had become exposed to His anger and judgment.

God asks them what happened and then imposed judgment. Eve was to have a desire for her husband whom she would have to listen to. She more importantly would then have increased pain in childbirth.

Adam would have to work the land for his food, no longer having it supplied for him by God.

The serpent would no longer be the larger creatures they were, walking and stalking the land for their food, feeding off the young and defenseless. They would crawl low and, on their bellies, as we see them today.

Satan planned to kill God's plan of coming and dwelling in His creation and use the new and favorite creature "man" to do it. The plan caused man to come under God's justice and be sentenced to death. This meant God would have to uphold His righteousness by killing His favorite creature.

But God is God and cannot be tricked. God instead suspended sentence for a time and allowed Himself to be the one on whom the sentence is imposed. Only by the sentence being imposed on mankind can this death penalty be fulfilled. But it could not be someone born with the sin already. One who is already infected with sin cannot cure it. Someone already convicted of a crime cannot take on the crimes and punishments of others. Any punishment would be solely applicable to their own transgressions. The only way to solve this was someone without any sin would have to take on the sins and punishments related to them, in this case it is whippings and finally the death penalty.

And so, the Messiah, the Son of God came and took on the death penalty which was imposed in Eden and added to by all the descendants of Adam and Eve. This removed the penalty of death for all who believe in this selfless sacrifice.

No one has greater love than this: that he lay down his life for his friends. (John 15:13 TLV)

"If you love Me, you will keep My commandments. (John 14:15 TLV)

So, God did this for us, His friends who obey His commands. Through this we become heirs of the Kingdom where He will reign forever.

The conclusion of it all

In summation, if you have read this far and have not thrown the book across the room proclaiming the author is mad, I thank you for your time and indulgence.

At the beginning of this it was mentioned about Biblical coincidences. The number of Biblical coincidences as shown just kept mounting up (and I know there are more). At what point do they cumulatively point to a truth? Is there a specific number which needs to be reached? Has this thesis reached that number?

All the points, all the obvious connections, the not so obvious ones, all the subtle and blatant parallels and types all can relate to that one common thread. One single action by Adam and Eve in the Garden runs straight through all of them.

This all came about when pondering how God's Triune nature is reflected in mankind. I was trying to understand some aspects of how human nature reflected God and came up with a conundrum. The woman, the representation of life somehow became representative of death. It didn't make sense. I could not reconcile it. I thought about it, asked God for some kind of understanding of it when suddenly one word flashed through my mind; "abortion". That is how the woman, the giver of life becomes bringer of death.

I leaned back as my eyes became wide open. It was like a rapid download as all the aspects of mankind's sinful history was explained. Murder, debt, wars, blood sacrifice, the Passover, Last Supper, Crucifixion and all those detailed in the Bible and now in this book all suddenly made sense. Everything fit. I began writing on my laptop, finishing four hours later in the wee hours of the morning.

I was shaking and had some tears in my eyes. I knew I had something to share. I discussed it with others as described earlier. The most telling was the person who was adamantly against it until the individual stopped to think about the implications. Finally admitting this may be correct.

Answering the questions

In the beginning of this the following questions were presented as needing to be answered.

- ✓ What did Adam and Eve do? *They killed the first born of creation*
- ✓ What kind of fruit was it? *It was the fruit of Eve's womb*
- ✓ Why did Satan take the form of a serpent? *They ate their own and other's young.*
- ✓ Why did Satan do it? *To prevent God from coming to dwell with man.*

- ✓ Why did Jesus / Yeshua have to die? *To take away the sin committed in Eden.*

- ✓ Why did He have to die the way He did? *To reflect and reverse what took place.*

- ✓ Why did the last days of Yeshua's life play out the way they did? *To undo what happened in Eden by reversing how it all took place.*

- ✓ How does the sinful act of Adam and Eve permeate all of subsequent human existence and actions such as wars, debt, greed and all the other sins mankind experiences? *It kills and feeds on the future instead of the future building on the present and past. Children are humanity's future.*

- ✓ How are the punishments appropriate to the crime? *Eve had increased pain in childbirth, Adam had to work for his food.*

The serpent became feared and loathsome

and forced to walk low, eating the dust.

✓ How could their act of sin affect all of

Creation itself?

He is the image of the invisible God, the firstborn of all creation. 16 For by Him all things were created, both in the heavens and on earth, visible and invisible, whether thrones or dominions or rulers or authorities—all things have been created through Him and for Him. 17 He is before all things, and in Him all things hold together. 18 He is also head of the body, the church; and He is the beginning, the firstborn from the dead, so that He Himself will come to have first place in everything. 19 For it was the Father's good pleasure for all the fullness to dwell in Him, 20 and through Him to reconcile all things to Himself, having made peace through the blood of His cross; through Him, I say, whether things on earth or things in heaven. (Colossians 1:15 NASB) o There is a lot in those verses which come to bear on the last of the questions posed.

o First, He (Yeshua) is the firstborn of all creation. Being the Firstborn has been covered.

o Second, by Him and through Him (Yeshua) all things were created.

o Third, He (Yeshua) holds all things together. This verse shows how the plan of the Adversary would affect all of creation, answering one of the underlying questions asked at the beginning of this book. How could their act of sin affect all of Creation itself?

These were the questions raised and answered. Along the way others came up as well and all were answered by the one word which was whispered to me that one late evening. All of those points in Scriptures listed and probably many more began as a result of the fall of Adam and Even in the Garden. The answer was a very simple, single answer to a host of questions which are all interrelated. There is no other answer which solves all of these questions. The more I study the Bible the more this answer presents itself as the singular event in human history which had the potential to prevent all of human history. It is the one and only action which had the potential to set in motion all the events which later happen as well as the way they happened.

This concept or thesis does not change anything about salvation or the need for faith and trust in Messiah as Savior. All it really does is explain what happened and why things played out the way they did.

More importantly, it can also point as a warning sign of our own situation today as we once again sacrifice the children for personal convenience. Over fifty million young and innocent lives and souls have been murdered in the United States alone since the legalization of this kind murder. No one has the choice to murder another person of any age. Like it or not, abortion is a form of murder.

Related to Today

This theological thesis puts forth the concept Eve and Adam killed a newborn child. They did it in much the same way "Partial Birth" abortions are practiced today, only they then started to eat thereof. As horrendous as this sounds, with this in mind, there is the direct connection this has to the numerous abortions going on today.

We may not be "eating" the aborted children, but it has been proven beyond any doubt those bodies are being cut and harvested for parts for sale on an open marketplace. A market stained with the blood of the sin of Eve and Adam. The same sin which began in Eden. Woman and Mankind have not changed in thousands of years no matter how much smarter or better we declare ourselves to be.

Today's society is so self-enamored and self-oriented it has proclaimed itself "enlightened" when in actuality it is in total darkness. Blinded by vanity, selfishness and personal expediency people will sacrifice anything to make their lives softer. Killing one's child is the epitome of such an attitude. Since abortion was legalized in the United States far over 50,000,000 (that's fifty MILLION) children have been murdered. Some may call it their right to choose, but no one has a right to choose to commit murder.

The premeditated act of killing one human being by another is the very definition of murder. The baby is a person with his or her own heart, his or her own brain, his or her own blood type and most especially his or her own very unique DNA, none of which are the mother's, or father's for that matter.

Some say it's just an "embryo" or similar term. But it's a term for a human being in the process of growing. So too are the terms "infant", "toddler", "child", "adolescent", "teen-ager", "young-adult" and other are all terms for a human being in different stages of growth. None of them make the individual any less a human being than another.

Yes, this thesis points to our continued performance of the Original Sin perpetrated in the Garden of Eden by Adam and Eve. It was not the intention of writing it, but it is the obvious conclusion. The sin was passed down generation after generation until it has reached a climax of untold proportions. These souls are now crying in heaven and not in their mother's arms. The final punishment for this sin has been pointed out. The people are cast out of their land. It has happened over and over again and will continue to do so until mankind learns and stops this barbaric practice. The slaughter of the innocent.

The Bible itself comes to a climactic point where Yeshua returns and reclaims the earth for his reign as sovereign. This was the intention in Eden at the beginning. God told the end from the beginning just as the Bible says. God will dwell with man.

There will be a new heaven and a new earth. Those who have sinned and have not repented will be removed, just as in the past. Adam and Eve were removed from the Garden. The people at the time of Noah were washed away. The people of the land of Canaan were removed and replaced by the Israelites. The Israelites were removed twice from their land. All this on account of sin. The same sin throughout, the thread which links them all together, the killing of the child. The killing of the future.

As noted, we commit this same sin today, not only in the act of abortion but in the continuation of various wars and debt. All feeding off the next generation for current self-comfort. A striking example is that of the Middle East terrorists who train their children to commit suicide. As the quote goes "when the Arabs love their children more than they hate ours we will have peace." This is exactly on point. It is a continuation of the Original Sin of humanity which began in Eden.

In the end, we must as a society realize we are not so enlightened. The ancients who we compare ourselves to, who we see as less enlightened than we, were doing exactly the same things we are doing today. Their methods may have varied, their weapons different, but the results were exactly the same. So too their reasons were the same as they are today, selfishness, vanity and comfort.

Sorry to say, mankind never learns a lesson until it's too late. Then when learned, after a few generations at most, we go right back to repeating the actions of our ancestors. Oddly, it's those who were spared the spike, burning flames, sacrificial altar and scalpel who perpetuate the sin. Just as Cain repeated the sin of murder, all these other generations up to the present time repeat the same murderous sin of infanticide. Mankind's heart has not changed. Mankind has certainly not become "enlightened".

The effects are self-evident in today's world. The woman has replaced her role as the bearer of life with that of the driving force for mankind's original sin. We cannot blame the man for committing the abortion, only the woman can make that final decision. One she is by all aspects of a civilized society, of all morality, not allowed to make. The destruction of the life of the family. The murder of another human being.

Today governments are making it legal to slaughter a child. Not shortly after conception but actually after the child is born. The doctor and the mother confer and decide whether or not to murder the child. Comedians are proclaiming they would have no problem eating an aborted fetus. What has happened to humanity? Does that word have any meaning at all anymore?

Are these not what this thesis is saying happened? We have come full circle. We have returned to the garden, only to commit the same sin all over again.

This will soon reach an apex and we will be driven from the land as has always been the case. Only this time the land may be the earth itself. Messiah will come, and judgment will once again be handed down. It's been shown it is inescapable.

In closing, once again I'd like to thank you for your time and consideration of this concept. Before making a final decision, give it some time to sink in, think about it, do not simply dismiss it out of hand.

As you read through the Scriptures, watch for both the glaring and subtle clues and evidence of what took place in Eden. It's all through the Bible as well as all through human existence, ancient and modern. It always rears its horrific head, sometimes glaringly, other times subtly. But it always shows up. The sin continues to rear its ugly head every day if one only pays attention to what is happening.

Keep studying the Scriptures, see for yourself. Keep the faith, He is coming sooner every day. Be well and be blessed.

Amen

As a final point, I feel it is necessary to mention "heresy". Some may see this thesis as being heretical. I do not take this concept lightly by any means. Which is why I went to great lengths to gather a great deal of Biblical support for the conclusion reached.

Heresy is defined as:

*1   a: adherence to **a religious opinion <u>contrary to church dogma</u>***

*   b: denial of a revealed truth by a baptized member of the Roman Catholic Church*

*   c: **an opinion or doctrine <u>contrary to church dogma</u>***

*2   a: **dissent or deviation from a dominant theory, opinion, or practice***

*   b: **<u>an opinion</u>**, doctrine, or practice **<u>contrary to</u>** the truth or to **<u>generally accepted beliefs or standards</u>***

Technically speaking, this thesis or discussion does seem to fit virtually all of the definitions above, so it can be considered "heresy" by the standards of "*Church Dogma*", "dominant theory, opinion or practice" and "generally accepted beliefs or standards".

I am definitely challenging so called "Church Dogma" and the "dominant theory". However, to be honest, on this particular subject, there is no specific dogma or a dominant theory. There is no concrete or overriding consensus of what took place in Eden. At the beginning the generally accepted beliefs were explained and shown to be nothing more than empty platitudes and vague suggestions. So this really is not heretical and may merely be theoretical. As the definition of "paradox" points out, it may be very well founded and potentially true.

It is a comfort to remember, when Yeshua was teaching He too was considered by many of the religious leadership to be teaching blasphemy and heresy.

Later it is written about the Bereans who when confronted with the Gospel, went back to the Scriptures and studied to confirm what they had heard. So I am in good company.

I truly feel the answer came from God through a whispered word of knowledge late one night. Later the title came to me with a word I had never used before "paradox". Piece by piece this work came together in ways I never expected. At least I can be thankful we're not burning people at the stake anymore.

The nursing child will play by the hole of the cobra, And the weaned child will put his hand on the viper's den.9 They will not hurt or destroy in all My holy mountain, For the earth will be full of the knowledge of the Lord As the waters cover the sea. (Isaiah 11:.8 NASB)

A Final Paradox?

As a final thought to all of this, something to ponder, there arose an interesting question or thought as this was completed. Consider these questions:

❖ Was there something else happening in the background we are not aware of? After all, we don't know everything God is doing.

❖ Was this all a trap for the Adversary?

❖ Was everything that happened in Eden continuing through to the eventual final end yet to come, all a set up by God?

No way to really know. To be honest, there's no writings in Scriptures I've found that points specifically to such a wild speculation. However, by a preponderance of the evidence, it may be concluded this to be a definite possibility, but certainly not definitive.

At first this was just mild speculation. It seemed like an interesting thought and nothing more. But then those pesky questions began popping up along with some very simple well-known answers which only served to solidify the questions.

- ❖ God knows everything ahead of time, He is "omniscient", therefore He had to know what would transpire.

- ❖ God would have known what was in Satan's heart or mind, again His Omniscience.

- ❖ God as pointed out earlier is a god of Justice and Righteousness, therefore a righteous judgment is required. This means a trial.

- ❖ People have free will, the ability to decide between right and wrong, whether to obey God or not.

- ❖ Are we, humanity the jury in the trial of the fallen angels?

Mankind was created with free will, to choose right from wrong. Angels on the other hand were not. They don't have such a luxury or curse for that matter as some may say. The question is, why not? Why are we made so much different with this self-destructive aspect of free will?

Since the overall angelic body is without the same free will, they cannot decide freely. This then begs the question, are we therefore the testing ground, the "court" so to speak which will decide the ultimate fate of the fallen?

If we once again consider the book of Enoch, of how mankind calls upon the Most High to hear our case, we can see a trial is being called for. Humanity is the accuser, the plaintiff. The Adversary and his legions are the defendants. But how do you have a fair trial when all the jury would be completely subject to the will of the judge?

Is this all to justly and fairly try the Adversary "Satan" and his fallen cohorts?

God would need to make man with free will, able to choose or not choose God's Will if so desired.

People have always wondered what mankind's purpose is, why are we here, why are we created the way we are. This may be the reason or at least one of them. After the final outcome, God will then create a new heaven and earth for He and His people to live together.

With the possibility it is or was a set up or trap for Satan and his cohorts?

How will you decide? Who do you stand with?

In the long run, and more importantly for us as children of the Most High God, our individual decisions carry more than just the fate of the Adversary and the fallen angels should such a speculation be true. Our decisions affect our own personal eternities. Regardless of all this possibly being a preplanned trap or trial or whatever, our duty is to worship the Lord with all our heart, soul and

body.

> *If it seems bad to you to worship Adonai,*
> *then choose for yourselves today whom*
> *you will serve—whether the gods that your*
> *fathers worshipped that were beyond the*
> *River or the gods of the Amorites in whose*
> *land you are living. But as for me and my*
> *household, we will worship Adonai!"*
> *(Joshua 24:15 TLV)*

As it was said in the movie "Indiana Jones and the

Last Crusade": *"It's time to ask yourself, what you believe"*.

Just something to think about; thank you again for

your time, patience and interest.

Credits

Cover design by D.B. Evans

Photo by Eddie Anastasio; Ephemera Photograhics
https://www.ephemeraphotographics.com/

Bibliography

Suggested books

Multiple translations of the Bible, (don't rely on just one)

Josephus' writings on the Jewish histories

Return of the Kosher Pig, by Yitzak Shapira

"Hebrew Word Pictures" by Dr. Frank T Seekins

Strong's Exhaustive Concordance,

The Project Gutenberg EBook of The Wars of the Jews or History of the

Destruction of Jerusalem, by Flavius Josephus www.gutenberg.org

Other Books by D. B. Evans:

The Sin Paradox, Amicus Brief

See It Believe It, A Guide to Teaching the Gospel in New Ways

Finding God, A Leisure Time Paradox